Delivering Quality in the NHS 2004

Edited by

Sir Michael Rawlins

Chairman
National Institute for Clinical Excellence

and

Peter Littlejohns

Clinical Director
National Institute for Clinical Excellence

Radcliffe Medical Press
Oxford • San Francisco

Radcliffe Medical Press Ltd
18 Marcham Road
Abingdon
Oxon OX14 1AA
United Kingdom

www.radcliffe-oxford.com
The Radcliffe Medical Press electronic catalogue and online ordering facility.
Direct sales to anywhere in the world.

———————————————————

British Library Cataloguing in Publication Data

A catalogue record for this book is available from the British Library.

ISBN 1 85775 618 5

Typeset by Acorn Bookwork, Salisbury, Wiltshire
Printed and bound by TJ International Ltd, Padstow, Cornwall

T

**This book is to be returned on or before
the last date stamped below.**

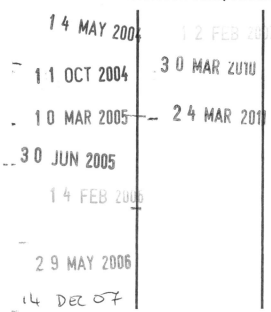

1 4 MAY 2004   1 2 FEB 2007

1 1 OCT 2004   3 0 MAR 2010

1 0 MAR 2005   2 4 MAR 2011

3 0 JUN 2005

1 4 FEB 2006

2 9 MAY 2006

14 DEC 07

Contents

List of contributors   vii

List of abbreviations   xi

Introduction   xiv

Part One: The James Lind legacy   1

The James Lind legacy: the past – James Lind   3
Ian Jenkins

The James Lind legacy: the present – the relevance of his work today   5
Iain Chalmers

Part Two: Filling the evidence gap   9

Filling the evidence gap: how big is it?   11
Kent Woods

What approaches have been used in assessing health technologies?
The contribution of HTA to decision making   14
John Gabbay

Formulating consensus recommendations   18
Gillian C Leng, Michael Pearson and Fergus Macbeth

What approaches have been used in assessing new interventional
procedures? A clinician's view   22
Trevor Cleveland

The role of patients and the public in generating research evidence   25
Sarah Buckland

MATCH: a role for academia and major research funders in generating
research evidence   28
Terry Young

Part Three: Raising standards – national policy and practice   33

Social care and joint working with the NHS: how the Social Care
Institute for Excellence works with NHS partners   35
Amanda Edwards and Patricia Kearney

The impact of emergency care targets on the quality agenda   38
K George MM Alberti

Progressive quality management: creating sustainable changes in
professional practice   40
Jon Harvey

Confidential Enquiry into Maternal and Child Health   43
Richard Congdon

The National Confidential Inquiry into Suicide and Homicide by People
with Mental Illness: recent findings and new directions   47
Nicola Swinson and Navneet Kapur

Raising standards in primary care   51
David Colin-Thomé

Measuring clinical performance   55
Jake Arnold-Forster

Four nations delivering a National Health Service   58
John Hill-Tout

Inspecting the private sector   61
Ros Gray

The Task Force on Medicines Partnership: implementing concordance
in medicine taking   64
Joanne Shaw and Geraldine Mynors

Partners for change? The impact of service user participation on
change and improvement in social care services   69
Sarah Carr

Part Four: Making a difference locally   75

Using CHI reviews to create a 'best practice' clinical audit department   77
Richard W Kuczyc

Working together to manage risk   82
Sarah Williamson

A strategic approach to clinical governance   85
Charlette Middlemiss

Reducing health inequalities   92
Paul Seviour

Making clinical governance work at the front line   95
Sean O'Kelly

National Clinical Audit 2002–2004   98
Jenifer Smith

Using patient and public involvement to improve the quality agenda
at a local level   102
Damian Jenkinson

Local mental health commissioning: issues and practice   106
Ian Allured and John Hall

Implementing NICE guidance: a partnership approach   109
Mary McClarey and Andy Dickens

A pocket guide to clinical governance   112
Kim Jelphs and Mike Cooke

Putting patient advocacy into practice: learning from Wales   118
Peter Johns

Quality improvements through nursing innovations   120
Jackie Dodds

Phase 2 Cardiac Rehabilitation Pilot Programme: Leeds North West PCT   123
Sue Kendal

Action on ENT: Blackburn's experience   126
Sarah Fitch

Facing up to failure: the impact of the star ratings   132
Jeremy Berger and Phil Glanfield

The Commission for Health Improvement: putting recommendations
into practice   135
Paul Bates

The implementation of NICE Technology Appraisal Guidance within
a cancer centre   138
Diana Mort, Carol Jordan and Gill Williams

2003 audit of NICE guidelines for the use of electronic fetal monitoring
at the Princess Anne Hospital, Southampton University Hospitals
NHS Trust   142
*Sucheta Iyengar, Patricia Norman, Suzanne Cunningham and
Matthew Coleman*

Developing your skills and enhancing your career   149
John Whitmore

Part Five: Research, evidence and recommendations   153

Involving participants in the design and conduct of trials: the
ProtecT study   155
Jenny Donovan

How the pharmaceutical industry gets patients involved in clinical
trials   158
Carol Aliyar

Consumer involvement in trial design and management 162
Mark Pitman

Mix and match? Conjectures on heterogeneous trial populations 165
H Martyn Evans

The Interventional Procedures Programme 168
Bruce Campbell and Tom Dent

What is the role of research and evidence in policy making? 171
Martin Eccles

What is the role of research and evidence in cancer policy? 176
Robert Haward

The role of evidence in improving market access 181
Julia Earnshaw

The role of health economics in making recommendations to the NHS 185
Martin Buxton

NICE challenges 188
Alan Maynard

Priority setting and healthcare commissioning: is there a case for
a UK network? 191
Angela Bate, Cam Donaldson and Tony Hope

Who has the responsibility for picking up the research agenda? 196
Chris Counsell

Index 199

List of contributors

K George MM Alberti, National Director for Emergency Access, Department of Health, London

Carol Aliyar, Head of Clinical Research Operations, Boehringer Ingelheim, Bracknell, Berkshire

Ian Allured, Service Development Advisor, Health and Social Care Advisory Service, London

Jake Arnold-Forster, Managing Director, Dr Foster Ltd, London

Angela Bate, Research Associate (Health Economics), Centre for Health Services Research, School of Population and Health Sciences, University of Newcastle upon Tyne

Paul Bates, Chief Executive, Herefordshire PCT, Belmont, Hereford

Dr Jeremy Berger, Clinical Management Group Chair and Consultant Radiologist, Barnet and Chase Farm Hospitals, London

Sarah Buckland, Director, INVOLVE Support Unit, Eastleigh

Professor Martin Buxton, Director, Health Economics Research Group, Brunel University, Uxbridge

Professor Bruce Campbell, Chairman of the Interventional Procedures Advisory Committee, National Institute for Clinical Excellence, London

Sarah Carr, Research Analyst, Social Care Institute for Excellence (SCIE), London

Sir Iain Chalmers, Co-ordinator, The James Lind Initiative, Oxford

Dr Trevor Cleveland, Consultant Vascular Radiologist, Sheffield Vascular Institute, Northern General Hospital, Sheffield

Matthew Coleman, Consultant in Fetal Medicine, Southampton University Hospitals NHS Trust, Southampton General Hospital

Professor David Colin-Thomé, National Clinical Director for Primary Care, Department of Health, London

Richard Congdon, Chief Executive, Confidential Enquiry into Maternal and Child Health, London

Mike Cooke, Chief Executive, South Staffordshire Healthcare NHS Trust, Lichfield, Staffordshire

Dr Chris Counsell, R&D Manager, University Hospital Birmingham NHS Trust

Suzanne Cunningham, Consultant Midwife, Southampton University Hospitals NHS Trust, Southampton General Hospital

Dr Tom Dent, Programme Director, National Institute for Clinical Excellence, London

Andy Dickens, Research Assistant, Institute of Health Studies, University of Plymouth

Jackie Dodds, Assistant Director of Nursing, Greater Peterborough Primary Care Partnership, Peterborough

Professor Cam Donaldson, Health Foundation Professor of Health Economics, Centre for Health Services Research, School of Population and Health Sciences and The Business School (Economics), University of Newcastle upon Tyne

Professor Jenny Donovan, Professor of Social Medicine, Department of Social Medicine, University of Bristol

Julia Earnshaw, Director, Health Outcomes, GlaxoSmithKline UK, Uxbridge

Professor Martin Eccles, William Leech Professor of Primary Care Research and Professor of Clinical Effectiveness, Centre for Health Services Research, School of Population and Health Sciences, University of Newcastle upon Tyne

Amanda Edwards, Head of Knowledge Services, Social Care Institute for Excellence, London

Professor H Martyn Evans, Professor of Humanities in Medicine, Centre for Arts and Humanities in Health and Medicine and Centre for Integrated Healthcare Research, University of Durham

Sarah Fitch, Nurse Practitioner – Nurse Advisor to Action on ENT Team, Blackburn Royal Infirmary, Blackburn

Professor John Gabbay, Director, National Collaborating Centre for Health Technology Assessment, University of Southampton

Phil Glanfield, Director, Performance Development Team, NHS Modernisation Agency

Ros Gray, Clinical Director, Nuffield Hospitals, Surbiton, Surrey

Dr John Hall, Clinical Advisor, Health and Social Care Advisory Service, London

Jon Harvey, Senior Fellow in Organisational Development, Office for Public Management, London

Professor Robert Haward, Professor of Cancer Studies, Centre for Epidemiology and Health Services Research, School of Medicine, University of Leeds

John Hill-Tout, Director of Performance Quality and Regulation – Health and Social Care, Welsh Assembly Government, NHS Performance Quality and Regulation Division, Cardiff

Professor Tony Hope, Director, Ethox, Institute of Health Sciences, University of Oxford

Dr Sucheta Iyengar, Research Fellow (Obstetrics), Southampton University Hospitals NHS Trust, Southampton General Hospital

Surgeon Vice Admiral Ian Jenkins, Surgeon General, Defence Medical Services, Ministry of Defence, London

Dr Damian Jenkinson, Clinical Director of Stroke Services, Royal Bournemouth and Christchurch Hospitals NHS Trust and Principal Clinical Advisor to the NHS Clinical Governance Support Programme for Stroke

Kim Jelphs, Clinical Director, South Staffordshire Healthcare NHS Trust, Clinical Development Directorate, Lichfield, Staffordshire

Peter Johns, Director Designate, Board of Welsh Community Health Councils, Cardiff

Carol Jordan, Registered General Nurse and Clinical Change Facilitator, Velindre NHS Trust, Whitchurch, Cardiff

Navneet Kapur, Assistant Director, National Confidential Inquiry into Suicide and Homicide by People with Mental Illness, Centre for Suicide Prevention, Manchester

Patricia Kearney, Director of Practice Development, Social Care Institute for Excellence, London

Sue Kendal, Coronary Heart Disease Nurse Specialist, Leeds North West PCT, Leeds

Richard W Kuczyc, Clinical Audit Manager, Portsmouth NHS Hospitals Trust, Portsmouth

Dr Gillian C Leng, Guidelines Programme Director, National Institute for Clinical Excellence, London

Dr Fergus Macbeth, Director, National Collaborating Centre for Cancer, Velindre NHS Trust, Cardiff

Alan Maynard, Professor of Health Economics, Department of Health Sciences, University of York

Mary McClarey, Head of Development, Research and Education, Plymouth Teaching Primary Care Trust, Mount Gould Hospital, Plymouth

Charlette Middlemiss, Clinical Governance Co-ordinator, Bro Morgannwg NHS Trust, Bridgend

Dr Diana Mort, Clinical Oncologist, Clinical Governance Lead and Director of Clinical Effectiveness/Audit Department, Velindre NHS Trust, Whitchurch, Cardiff

Geraldine Mynors, Head of Projects, The Task Force on Medicines Partnership, London

Patricia Norman, Clinical Effectiveness Co-ordinator, Southampton University Hospitals NHS Trust, Southampton General Hospital

Dr Sean O'Kelly, Consultant Anaesthetist and Deputy Medical Director, Great Western Hospital, Swindon and National Clinical Lead, NHS Modernisation Agency Associates, London

Dr Michael Pearson, Director, National Collaborating Centre for Chronic Conditions, London

Dr Mark Pitman, Research Programme Manager, Medical Research Council, London

Dr Paul Seviour, General Practitioner, North Somerset PCT, Weston-Super-Mare

Joanne Shaw, Director, The Task Force on Medicines Partnership, London

Dr Jenifer Smith, Head of Clinical Audit, Commission for Health Improvement, London

Dr Nicola Swinson, Clinical Reseach Fellow, National Confidential Inquiry into Suicide and Homicide by People with Mental Illness, Centre for Suicide Prevention, Manchester

John Whitmore, Founding Partner, Performance Consultants, Leigh, Kent

Gill Williams, Clinical Audit Officer, Cancer Services, Velindre NHS Trust, Whitchurch, Cardiff

Sarah Williamson, Clinical Risk Manager, Sheffield Teaching Hospitals NHS Trust, Sheffield

Professor Kent Woods, Director, NHS Health Technology Assessment Programme, University of Leicester, Department of Cardiovascular Sciences, Leicester Royal Infirmary

Professor Terry Young, Multidisciplinary Assessment of Technology Centre for Health (MATCH) Consortium and Chair of Healthcare Systems, Brunel University, Uxbridge

List of abbreviations

ABPI	Association of The British Pharmaceutical Industry
ASL	active sick leave
AZT	zidovudine
BAMM	British Association of Medical Managers
BSE	bovine spongiform encephalopathy
CDM	chronic disease management
CEA	cost-effectiveness analysis
CEMACH	Confidential Enquiry into Maternal and Child Health
CEMD	Confidential Enquiry into Maternal Deaths
CESDI	Confidential Enquiry into Stillbirths and Deaths in Infancy
CHAI	Commisssion for Healthcare Audit and Inspection
CHC	community health council
CHD	coronary heart disease
CHI	Commission for Health Improvement
CJD	Creutzfeldt-Jakob disease
CMO	Chief Medical Officer
CPT	clinical process teams
CSCI	Commission for Social Care Inspection
CWP	Changing Workforce Programme
DNBI	disease and non-battle injury
DoH	Department of Health
DTI	Department of Trade and Industry
EBM	evidence-based medicine
EFM	electronic fetal monitoring
ENT	ear, nose and throat
EPPI	Evidence for Policy and Practice Information (Centre)
EPSRC	Engineering and Physical Sciences Research Council
EU	European Union
FBS	fetal blood sampling
GDG	guideline development group
GMS	General Medical Services
GP	general practitioner
HASCAS	Health and Social Care Advisory Service
HICSS	hospital integrated clinical support system
HRT	hormone replacement therapy
HTA	Health Technology Assessment
IA	intermittent auscultation
IM&T	information technology and management

INAHTA	International Network of Agencies for Health Technology Assessment
IPAC	Interventional Procedures Advisory Committee
MANMED	Management of Medicines
MATCH	Multidisciplinary Assessment of Technology Centre for Health
MRC	Medical Research Council
NatPaCT	National Primary and Care Trust
NCASP	National Clinical Audit Support Programme
NCC	National Collaborating Centre
NCCHTA	National Collaborating Centre for Health Technology Assessment
NCSC	National Care Standards Commission
NHS SDO	NHS Service Delivery and Organisation Research and Development
NICE	National Institute for Clinical Excellence
NICE TAG	NICE Technology Appraisal Guidance
NIMHE	National Institute for Mental Health in England
NPDT	National Primary Care Development Team
NSF	National Service Framework
ONS	Office for National Statistics
PACT	Patients' Attitudes to Clinical Trials
PALS	patient advice and liaison services
PCO	primary care organisation
PCT	primary care trust
PDSA	plan, do, study, act
PDT	Performance Development Trust
PEAT	patient environment action team
PFI	private finance initiative
PHCT	primary healthcare team
PMS	Personal Medical Services
PPI	patient and public involvement
ProtecT	prostate testing for cancer and treatment
PSA	prostate-specific antigen
PwSI	professional with a special interest
QALY	quality adjusted life year
QUIDS	quality indicators for diabetes services
R&D	research and development
RAID	review, agree, implement, demonstrate
RCN	Royal College of Nursing
SCIE	Social Care Institute for Excellence
sCJD	sporadic Creutzfeldt-Jakob disease
SERNIP	Safety and Efficacy Register for New Interventional Procedures
SHA	strategic health authority
TAR	technology assessment report
TSC	trial steering committee

vCJD	variant Creutzfeldt-Jakob disease
WDC	Workforce Development Confederation
WHO	World Health Organization

Introduction

Clinical Excellence 2003 was the fifth annual NICE conference. The event brings together a diverse group of people involved with healthcare, including clinicians, managers and patients: the people who are responsible for raising clinical standards in the NHS and for implementing best practice.

Those presenting papers at the Conference discussed not only the issues shaping the national healthcare agenda but also examples of best practice in action, giving delegates practical illustrations of how national policy can be implemented at a local level. 2003 was the 250th anniversary of the work of James Lind. The first day of the Conference discussed Lind's *Treatise of the scurvy*, widely recognised as the first published controlled trial and with a 'protocol' developed from a review of the existing literature. It is the foundation of evidence-based medicine.

This publication brings together papers from many of those who spoke at the Conference. It offers delegates the opportunity to refresh their memories and, for those who couldn't attend, a chance to sample some of the excellent learning that came from the event. These papers offer examples of the type of best practice that goes on throughout the NHS all the time. They demonstrate the excellence of the work undertaken by health professionals and academics who concern themselves with delivering quality and improving patient care. Many of the projects described can be adapted and applied at a local level.

I would like to take this opportunity to thank all those who made the Conference a success. Once again, feedback from the delegates has been excellent and we've received some very constructive comments that will help us to shape the programme for *Clinical Excellence 2004*. We look forward to seeing you then.

Michael Rawlins
Chairman, NICE
February 2004

PART ONE

The James Lind legacy

The James Lind legacy: the past – James Lind

Ian Jenkins

Disease and non-battle injury (DNBI) is one of the greatest challenges to armed forces' medical services on operations. DNBI has always been a major threat to force preparation, operational effectiveness and fighting capability and is not a new phenomenon.

As Britain broadened her overseas power and domination the Royal Navy extended its global reach; its lines of communication, support and provision became greatly stretched and a number of diseases emerged, not least of which was scurvy. This single condition seriously reduced the Navy's fighting capability and compromised Britain's maritime supremacy.

Scurvy was not a new disorder. It had been described by Hippocrates and the Egyptians and had compromised many campaigns throughout history. Indeed, Sir Richard Hawkins had observed, '... that which I have observed most fruitful for this sickness is sour oranges and lemons ...', and recommended their use as antiscorbutics in 1594. Captain Lancaster of the British East India Company used lemon juice as a preventative measure in 1601 and John Woodall, who became the company's surgeon-general in 1612, incorporated this advice in *The Surgeon's Mate* in 1617. Scurvy, however, devastated Commodore Anson's voyage round the world (1740–1744). Of nearly 2000 men in his squadron of six ships, more than 1000 failed to return. Only four died in action and the majority are thought to have died of scurvy or its adverse effect on their seamanship.

James Lind entered the Navy in 1739 as a 23-year-old surgeon's mate. He served in the Mediterranean, West Africa and the West Indies, and became surgeon to the fourth rate HMS *Salisbury* in 1746. He was moved by the number of cases of scurvy and was undoubtedly aware of the previous reports that fruit and vegetables could be beneficial, but was obviously frustrated by the confused, indecisive teaching and lack of knowledge.

On 20 May 1747 Lind selected 12 patients with scurvy on board HMS *Salisbury* at sea. In his words:

'Their cases were as similar as I could have them. They all in general had putrid gums, the spots and lassitude, with weakness of their knees. They lay together in one place, being a proper apartment for the sick in the fore-hold; and had one diet common to all …'

He randomised the patients into six pairs and prescribed a different daily regime to each pair: cider, elixir of vitriol, vinegar, seawater, oranges and lemons, and nutmeg.

The pair on oranges and lemons improved rapidly, one being fit for duty after only six days. There were no signs of improvement in the others despite continuing on their course of treatment for two weeks.

Lind left the Navy in 1748 and returned to Edinburgh to study for his MD, becoming a Fellow of the Royal College of Physicians of Edinburgh in 1750. His work on HMS *Salisbury* was published in 1753 as *A Treatise of the Scurvy, in Three Parts, Containing an Inquiry into the Nature, Causes, and Cure, of that Disease, Together with a Critical and Chronological View of what has been Published on the Subject*. As the title so eloquently reflects, it described his randomised, prospective clinical trial, probably the first of its kind, and consolidated the principles of systematic review and controlled clinical study. It was further expanded and improved and the third edition was published in London in 1772.

In 1758 Lind joined the Royal Hospital Haslar as physician and governor until relieved in 1783 by his son. He contributed to many other pioneering areas of preventive medicine and the health of the Navy, but despite his professional distinction he remained modest and unassuming and never achieved the fame, social status or knighthood enjoyed by some of his less talented successors. He died in July 1794.

Much has been said of the Navy's reluctance to recognise the value of Lind's work, including the treatment and prevention of scurvy, and it is largely believed that it was not until the influence of Sir Gilbert Blane that the Admiralty finally adopted his recommendations and introduced lemon juice into the Fleet in 1795 – a year after Lind's death!

Lind's recognition of the importance of systematic review, sound science and prospective clinical trial is as relevant today as it was in the 18th century, perhaps even more so in this age of commercialism and confused national and international medical ethics and law. Perhaps more important, however, was his direct influence on the fitness and fighting capability of the Royal Navy in the 18th and 19th centuries, which undoubtedly preserved British maritime superiority and the ability to defeat the French and Spanish navies. His influence on the physical fitness of British sailors made the Royal Navy the global battle-winning fleet of the day and is an excellent example of medicine influencing the course of history.

For this, James Lind became known as *The Father of Naval Medicine* and it is fitting that the crest of the Institute of Naval Medicine features the lemon tree.

The James Lind legacy: the present – the relevance of his work today

Iain Chalmers

James Lind's 1753 *Treatise of the Scurvy* is a classic for two main reasons:

1   his 'critical and chronological view' of what had been published on the diagnosis, prognosis, prevention and treatment of scurvy
2   his account of a prospectively controlled clinical experiment comparing six commonly used treatments for the disease.

The relevance of Lind's systematic review today

In the Preface to his *Treatise of the Scurvy*, Lind observed that 'before the subject could be set in a clear and proper light, it was necessary to remove a great deal of rubbish'. Accordingly, he gave details of his search strategy for relevant material, presented abstracts of previous reports and recorded his assessment of the reliability of observations made by earlier authors. Is sufficient attention paid today to the need for systematic reviews of research to inform decisions about clinical practice, healthcare policy, and future research?

Systematic reviews of research evidence are fundamental for the work of the National Institute for Clinical Excellence (NICE) and other organisations, and there has been an encouraging increase in rigorous research synthesis over the past decade. Substantial problems remain, however, partly because the science of research synthesis remains insufficiently recognised within academia.[1] The resulting problem is manifested in most reports of research: readers are usually unable to assess the contribution made by a new study to the overall evidence base because the results of new studies are only rarely presented in the context of systematic reviews of other relevant studies.[2]

Although the principal need of NICE and other organisations is for systematic reviews of research involving patients and the public, failure to prepare scientifi-

cally defensible reviews of pre-clinical research can also have adverse consequences for human beings. For example, a systematic review of the effects of a
calcium antagonist (nimodipine) in animal model experiments of focal cerebral
ischaemia has raised questions about whether it was ever justified to proceed to
controlled trials involving nearly 7000 patients.[3]

One consequence of the increase in scientifically defensible approaches to
research synthesis is that systematic reviews have exposed the pervasive
problem of failure to report disappointing results.[4] This, too, has serious implications for patients and the public. For example, in October 2002, for the first
time, the Medicines Control Agency withdrew product licences for evening
primrose oil supplements 'following a review of all the relevant information,
including new studies and statistical analyses'.[5] This action was taken because
the data did not support 'the current standard of efficacy required for authorisation of these products for the treatment of eczema and mastalgia'.

In fact, eight years previously, the Department of Health commissioned a
systematic review of evening primrose oil in eczema, which failed to find any
evidence to support the NHS's sizeable investment in the drug. This information
was not made public at the time, however, because the manufacturers threa-
tened to sue if a report of the review was published, as it included previously
unpublished 'negative' data supplied in confidence. Decisions not to report
clinical research because the findings threaten vested interests other than the
interests of users of the NHS are unacceptable on both scientific and ethical
grounds.[6] NICE and other organisations are in a strong position to reduce this
form of misconduct.

The relevance of Lind's controlled clinical experiment today

In addition to his systematic review of the work of other investigators and
writers, James Lind confronted his uncertainty about how to treat scurvy by
conducting a prospectively controlled clinical trial, as an uncontentious element
of his normal clinical practice. What are the responsibilities of today's healthcare professionals and policy makers when they are uncertain about which
among alternative treatments or policies to recommend for their patients or the
public?

If uncertainty remains after taking account of the findings of systematic
reviews, local circumstances and personal preferences, clinical practice and
policy implementation should be organised in ways designed to reduce uncertainty and provide better evidence to inform future decisions.[7] This principle
has been endorsed implicitly by all professionals and patients who have participated in randomised controlled trials. Indeed, many of them appear to want the
principle to be applied more widely. The principle has sometimes also been
endorsed explicitly by the NHS, for example when access to extracorporeal
membrane oxygenation for neonatal asphyxia was restricted to babies treated

within the context of a randomised controlled trial.[8] NICE, too, after reviewing the available evidence on the effects of healthcare interventions, has sometimes recommended that they be used only within the context of randomised trials, but it is unclear to what extent clinical and research governance have been able to ensure that these injunctions have been observed.[9,10]

As the first director of the NHS Health Technology Assessment (HTA) Programme has observed, 'with 60 million people in this country all using the NHS, the opportunities to answer questions quickly if everybody collaborates is unique'.[11] However, there are now formidable obstacles confronting anyone wishing to promote the principle of addressing uncertainty by formal evaluation within usual clinical practice.

A longstanding problem concerns the unethical promotion of a double standard in respect of informed consent to treatment: clinicians are expected to seek permission if they want to give a treatment to half their patients (and reduce uncertainties about its effects), but not if they decide to acquiesce in uncertainty and give the same treatment to all of their patients.[12–14]

Within the UK, these double standards have been exacerbated by the effects of an incompetent government enquiry into allegations of research misconduct in North Staffordshire NHS Trust, which government spokesmen continue to refer to as if evidence of research misconduct had been uncovered.[15,16] Unsurprisingly in the face of government unwillingness to admit the limitations of this influential enquiry (it led to the NHS Research Governance Framework), it continues to cast a pall over efforts to evaluate clinical practice.[17]

More recently, those who wish to see uncertainties about the effects of treatments and policies addressed as a normal and expected element of usual clinical practice find that they are frustrated by additional barriers resulting from European legislation on privacy and clinical trials. As if these disincentives to embedding rigorous evaluation within clinical practice in the NHS were not enough, the prospects of applying this principle have been further reduced by a decline in the numbers of randomised trials supported by the principal non-commercial sources of funds (particularly the NHS Research and Development Programme), inadequate infrastructure and trained personnel, and an unwillingness within academia to recognise the importance of the collaborative work on which reliable evaluation of clinical practice often depends.[18,19]

James Lind's controlled comparison of different treatments for scurvy is often regarded as the first controlled trial. Two hundred and fifty years after he published the report of his study, the future of non-commercial controlled trials within the NHS looks bleak.

References

1   Alderson P, Gliddon L and Chalmers I (2003) Academic recognition of critical appraisal and systematic reviews in British postgraduate medical education. *Medical Education* 37: 386–7.

2   Clarke M, Alderson P and Chalmers I (2002) Discussion sections in reports of controlled trials published in general medical journals. *Journal of the American Medical Association* **287**: 2799–801.

3   Sandercock P and Roberts I (2002) Systematic reviews of animal experiments. *Lancet* **2**: 586.

4   Dickersin K (1997) How important is publication bias? A synthesis of available data. *AIDS Education and Prevention* **9 (Suppl 1)**: 15–21.

5   Medicines Control Agency (2002) *What's New: Epogam and Efamast (gamolenic acid): withdrawal of marketing authorisation.* www.mca.gov.uk/whatsnew/epogam.htm

6   Antes G and Chalmers I (2003) Under-reporting of clinical trials is unethical. *Lancet* **361**: 978–9.

7   Chalmers I (2000) It's official: evaluative research must become part of routine care in the NHS. *Journal of the Royal Society of Medicine* **93**: 555–6.

8   UK Collaborative ECMO Trial Group (1996) UK collaborative randomised trial of neonatal extracorporeal membrane oxygenation. *Lancet* **2**: 75–82.

9   National Institute for Clinical Excellence (2000) *Guidance on the Use of Autologous Cartilage Transplantation for Full Thickness Cartilage Defects in Knee Joints.* NICE Technology Appraisal Guidance No. 16, December 2000.

10 National Institute for Clinical Excellence (2000) *Guidance on the Use of Laparoscopic Surgery for Colorectal Cancer.* NICE Technology Appraisal Guidance No. 17, December 2000.

11 Irving M (2000) Summing up. In: K Johnston and J Sussex (eds) *Surgical Research and Development in the NHS.* Office of Health Economics: London, pp. 99–105.

12 Oxman AD, Chalmers I and Sackett DL (2001) A practical guide to informed consent to treatment. *British Medical Journal* **323**: 1464–6.

13 Glasziou P and Chalmers I (2004) Ethics review roulette: what can we learn? *British Medical Journal* **328**: 121–2.

14 Smithells RW (1975) Iatrogenic hazards and their effects. *Postgraduate Medical Journal* **15**: 39–52.

15 Hey E and Chalmers I (2000) Investigating allegations of research misconduct: the vital need for due process. *British Medical Journal* **321**: 752–6.

16 Lord Davies of Oldham (2003) *Clinical Trials: EU Directive.* Hansard 10, September 2003, Column 289.

17 Nicklin SE and Spencer SA (in press) Recruitment failure in early neonatal research. *Archives of Diseases in Childhood.*

18 Chalmers I, Rounding C and Lock K (2003) Non-commercial randomized controlled trials in the UK, 1980–2002: a survey. *British Medical Journal* **327**: 1017–19.

19 Bell J (2003) Resuscitating clinical research in the UK. *British Medical Journal* **327**: 1041–3.

PART TWO

Filling the evidence gap

Filling the evidence gap: how big is it?

Kent Woods

The recent growth of evidence-based medicine has focused mainly on the efficacy of healthcare interventions. Similarly, the emphasis of appraisal, leading to national guidance for the NHS, has been predominantly on individual technologies. The evidence base underpinning appraisal has been the assessment of effectiveness and cost-effectiveness of these interventions. Methodological development has been directed towards combating bias and reducing uncertainty around the point estimates of clinical and cost-effectiveness. These can be considered to be aspects of 'therapeutic uncertainty'.

Clinical decision making has a somewhat different perspective. Its starting point is the individual patient and the diagnosis for which intervention is being considered. There are, therefore, three classes of uncertainty:

1   diagnostic uncertainty
2   prognostic uncertainty
3   therapeutic uncertainty.

They are addressed sequentially. Until a diagnostic and a prognostic category have been assigned, it is not possible to apply estimates of therapeutic effectiveness and cost-effectiveness to the individual patient. Put simply, we need to apply an accurate label which can be related to the samples of patients who have been included in the studies of individual technologies. We also need to ensure that the likely prognosis for the individual corresponds to the categories of prognosis tht have been included in therapeutic studies – the 'case mix'. Unless these steps are carried out explicitly, the population outcomes of treatment will not replicate the sample estimates which have been derived from clinical trials. This will apply equally to clinical outcomes and to health-economic outcomes.

This will be illustrated by a series of examples from a range of clinical settings. In some instances there have been efforts to resolve diagnostic and prognostic uncertainty, but in others very little has been achieved. For the latter, the public health impact of the available technologies will be highly uncertain until therapeutic trials are supported by further research – often epidemiological – to clarify the diagnostic and prognostic uncertainties faced in clinical practice.

Heart failure

Heart failure is conventionally identified by the symptoms of fatigue and exertional breathlessness and by signs of pulmonary congestion and peripheral oedema. None of these is sensitive or specific for the diagnosis. Clinical trials of treatments for heart failure have generally applied imaging technologies such as echocardiography to confirm and quantify impaired ventricular function, but these have only recently become available in the community and are not universally used. The public health impact of effective treatments for heart failure is therefore hard to estimate because of diagnostic and prognostic uncertainty in the clinical population receiving treatment. The general introduction of assays for natriuretic peptides may be of considerable benefit for both diagnosis and prognosis, but will create a new classification system by which to describe the samples of patients included in therapeutic trials.

Major depression

Antidepressants have mainly been assessed in patients with major depression of moderate to severe degree. They are widely used in milder forms of depression, for which their therapeutic effectiveness is less certain, and for disturbances of mood which do not satisfy diagnostic criteria for depression. Here the extrapolation from clinical effectiveness to public health impact is compromised by both diagnostic and prognostic uncertainty for which there is no easily applicable clinical tool.

Abdominal aortic aneurysm

Abdominal aortic aneurysm is relatively easy to diagnose by ultrasound once clinical suspicion has been raised. Its prognosis is related to the diameter of the dilated aortic segment. Substantial research has been done to quantify the link between aneurysm diameter and risk of rupture (i.e. prognosis) and therefore the relative benefit of intervention either by open aneurysm repair or (currently being assessed) stent graft insertion. In this instance, the main barrier to extrapolation of therapeutic effectiveness data to public health impact is diagnostic uncertainty arising from the clinically silent course of the condition in most patients. Population screening would be necessary to close this knowledge gap.

Hypercholesterolaemia

Hypercholesterolaemia as a risk marker for cardiovascular events is increasingly used as an indication for drug intervention in the asymptomatic population. The therapeutic effectiveness of statins is based on strong trials evidence in both primary and secondary prevention. However, prognosis for the individual at any given level of cholesterol is strongly determined by other determinants of cardiovascular risk, such as smoking habit, blood pressure, diabetes or impaired glucose tolerance, family history, sex and age. It is now standard practice to estimate individual prognosis using multivariate methods before starting statin treatment. Here the 'diagnosis' of cholesterol level is technically simple but the prognostic uncertainty relates to a cluster of factors of which cholesterol level is only one. Therapeutic uncertainty for statins has been substantially reduced by therapeutic trials carried out in large numbers of patients across a wide range of cholesterol levels and levels of cardiovascular risk. However, the relative therapeutic effectiveness of alternative approaches to reducing cardiovascular risk remains uncertain – for example smoking cessation, exercise, weight reduction, blood pressure reduction and/or cholesterol reduction. Clinicians and patients must negotiate a strategy which is likely to be feasible, effective, cost-effective and acceptable in the face of residual therapeutic uncertainty.

Discussion

The last two examples illustrate the particular complexities of clinical decision making when the aim is to reduce the risk of future events rather than to improve the clinical outcome of current disease states, i.e. 'prevention' rather than 'treatment' in conventional terminology. It is important to retain clarity on the distinction and on the components of diagnostic, prognostic and therapeutic uncertainty. The necessary evidence base extends beyond clinical trials. It must include epidemiological (quantitative observational) studies to define prevalence and natural history of the target conditions, whether these be 'diseases' or risk factors for disease. Clinical trials to show efficacy must be complemented by robust observational research to confirm clinical effectiveness in the target population. The rudimentary nature of audit for most NHS activities is a major gap in the evidence base for decision makers. Filling this gap will require major efforts in our conceptual understanding of disease and risk of disease, in the capture of reliable data as an integral part of providing health services and in the systematic analysis of risk-adjusted outcomes in relation to interventions delivered.

What approaches have been used in assessing health technologies? The contribution of HTA to decision making

John Gabbay

Health technology assessment (HTA) is a key part of the conduit between clinical research and policy making. Seeking to bring together all the available relevant and reliable evidence about the appropriateness of a healthcare intervention, it is a scientific endeavour in its own right, using replicable and often complex methods to obtain generalisable results. But the assessment is also designed specifically to inform policy decisions about the use of those technologies at the macro- (e.g. an entire health system), the meso- (e.g. a local provider) and the micro-level (e.g. individual patient decisions). Occupying this middle ground between science and policy presents many special challenges.

Even before one begins an assessment, there is the problem of selecting which of the thousands of existing and emerging health technologies to assess, as only a minority will repay the effort, in terms of potential influence on healthcare policy, of undertaking an assessment. Then one needs to agree the precise questions about, say, the cost-effectiveness that will need to be answered in order to best inform those who are deciding whether or not to use that intervention. It is no easy task even to scope the technical questions (for example, which version of the technology to assess, used in what way, by which subset of professionals, at what stage of its development, for which indications, in which precise group of patients, in which healthcare sector, applying what costings?). Once these questions have been agreed, there is the need to ensure that the HTA methodology is robust, which is perhaps why 62/417 (15%) of the assessments commissioned by the NHS HTA programme since it began in 1993 have been projects designed to develop the methodology of both secondary (systematic reviews and modelling) and primary (complex trials and other methods) research to assess health technologies. Finally, because HTA has a unique relationship to policy, the art and science of implementation requires a different approach from the implementation of more conventional clinical or health services research.

Since it began its work in 1999, NICE – now the most influential policy-forming body for the NHS – has been closely aligned to the HTA programme. For example, NICE's clinical guidelines programme has made much use of HTA findings. But it is in the appraisals programme where, as NICE chairman Sir Michael Rawlins has recently stated, 'from the outset the NHS's HTA programme has played a critical role in both setting NICE's agenda (from previous reports) and supporting our appraisals programme. The quality of the Institute's appraisals ... would never have been achieved without it.' An example of a such a pre-existing HTA, which was identified as a high priority topic very early in the HTA programme and which later influenced policy through NICE, was a systematic review of hip replacements. This led to one of the first pieces of NICE guidance in 2000, potentially saving the NHS up to £8 million per year by recommending the prostheses with the lowest documented failure rates.

The Department of Health (DoH) has formalised HTA's role in underpinning policy by setting up a system whereby the NICE appraisals programme relies on assessments directly provided under contract by the HTA programme. This relies on a clear distinction between 'assessment' and 'appraisal'. Appraisal, carried out by the NICE appraisal committees, is a judgement based on assessment but also incorporating wider views about relative priority, equity, accept-

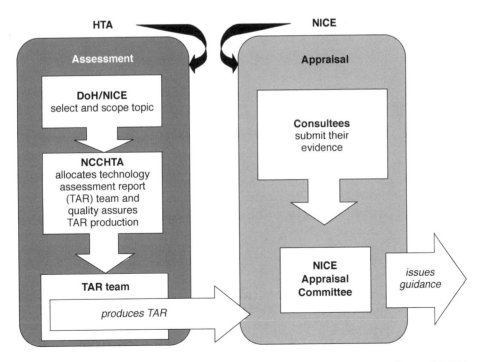

Figure A The relationship between HTA and NICE appraisals. NCCHTA: National Collaborating Centre for Health Technology Assessment.

ability and feasibility of the technology; in contrast to assessment, appraisals will not be generalisable but will always be specific to a particular context. The relationship between HTA-led assessment and NICE-led appraisal is illustrated in Figure A, which also shows how appraisal must take account not only of the synthesis of research evidence from HTA, but of other influences from a wide range of key stakeholders.

In the UK, where the assessment/appraisal distinction has been most clearly delineated, most HTA rests on research evidence about efficacy, effectiveness and/or cost-effectiveness – often expressed as cost per quality adjusted life year (QALY). But what about the many other factors that affect the decision whether to use a healthcare intervention or not? Across the world there are now over 40 public sector agencies producing a stream of HTAs to inform their governments and payers. In many of them, but not yet in the UK, assessment goes beyond clinical, epidemiological and economic assessment to include detailed objective analyses of the ethical, social and organisational implications of new technology. A recent survey by the International Network of Agencies for HTA (INAHTA) showed that 14% always include ethical analyses in their HTAs, 56% have sometimes included them and 14% never include them. The fact that there are such differing views about the remit of HTA is another demonstration of the distinctive role of HTA. As a science designed to inform policy, HTA will inevitably be tailored to the way that decisions are made in a given health

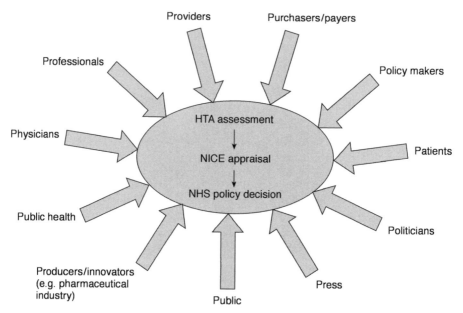

Figure B Perspectives and pressures on the processes from HTA to policy decision making.

system, where there will always be pressures from a very wide range of potential sources, at whatever level one is working. At the micro-level of individual patient decisions, however sound the research evidence may be, it will be tempered by clinical judgement about an individual patient. And at the macro- and meso-levels, policy makers need to juggle and balance pressures from a wide range of key players (*see* Figure B). Policy making is ultimately the art of the possible, not the science of the QALY.

HTA may find that it is sowing the seeds of frustration among decision makers by confining itself to clinical and economic research evidence while failing to provide support for these complex balancing acts. By having so successfully established the analysis of research evidence as an essential component of NHS policy making, HTA may have highlighted the need for similarly systematic analyses of the contextual and other related aspects of the technology – as indeed a recent internal review of the NICE appraisal system has suggested. A victim of its own success, HTA may be called on to reinvent itself as a provider of much broader analyses of which there has been little or no experience in the UK. In continuing to develop its role as the conduit between science and policy making, HTA may need to adopt a more sophisticated understanding of different types of evidence in decision making, and to broaden its skill mix to encompass them. Is it up to the challenge?

Formulating consensus recommendations

Gillian C Leng, Michael Pearson and Fergus Macbeth

Introduction

Clinical guidelines are recommendations, based on the best available evidence, for the care of individuals by healthcare professionals. They are defined as 'systematically developed statements designed to assist practitioner and patient on decisions about appropriate healthcare for specific clinical circumstances', although they are also relevant to NHS managers and patients. Guideline recommendations are formulated by a representative group of 12–15 healthcare professionals, patients and methodologists. They examine the best evidence available to answer a particular question, and generate a recommendation by a process of informal consensus. The group leader is essential to this process, and facilitates consensus by setting clear rules for group functioning, by establishing a climate of trust and mutual respect between members, and by encouraging constructive debate involving all members. In some areas, however, the group may be unable to reach consensus through this process, often because the evidence base is so limited that it adds little to the decision making. In these situations, more formal methods of reaching consensus may be applied. This paper briefly describes types of formal consensus used in the NICE clinical guidelines programme, including novel systems piloted at the National Collaborating Centres for Chronic Conditions and Cancer.

Methods of formal consensus in guideline development

There are three main methods of formal consensus regularly used in healthcare and guideline development: the Delphi technique, the nominal group technique and the consensus development conference. Each has its own advantages and shortcomings. Their use should be tailored to the needs of the guideline development group, the types of questions to be answered and also the time available, as the techniques can be very detailed and time intensive. Often people use hybrids of the methods to make the work more manageable. The composition of a group of individuals selected for formal consensus should reflect the full range of characteristics of those they are trying to represent. A homogeneous group will reach greater consensus, because specialists tend to favour the interventions/views with which they are familiar, but such a group may not be wholly representative of the healthcare workers whose practice is being addressed in the guideline, and is unlikely to represent the views of patients. There is evidence that a consensus group of 10–12 people is probably sufficient to allow conclusions to be reached, as including more people seems to have little effect on the conclusions reached by the group.[1] In most cases, therefore, the guideline development group itself will fulfil the requirements for a consensus group.

The nominal group technique

The nominal group technique uses a variety of postal (or computer) and face-to-face techniques to elicit a consensus view. First, individual participants record their ideas independently and privately. The ideas are collected in turn from individuals and are fed back to the group when they are brought together for discussion, followed by a further private vote. The National Collaborating Centre (NCC) for Acute Care has used a modified nominal group technique to identify areas of agreement in the development of the clinical guideline on routine pre-operative testing (details on the NICE website www.nice.org.uk). This was a topic area where there was an extremely limited evidence base, and the formal consensus process was used to develop robust recommendations.

Novel approaches to formal consensus

The Pearson Process for consensus development

The Pearson Process has been developed at the NCC for Chronic Conditions. The method uses a hybrid of the Delphi and nominal group techniques, and is assisted by electronic voting to document decisions. A representative group of 25–30 individuals (including those on the guideline development group) meet to discuss and agree the final version of a clinical guideline. This group is asked to:

- confirm recommendations based on good evidence
- approve recommendations based on lesser evidence or extrapolations from other situations
- reach consensus recommendations where evidence is inadequate.

The draft guideline is sent to the group, accompanied by an electronic spread-sheet inviting each person to vote on a nine-point Likert scale ranging from strong agreement to strong disagreement. The spreadsheets are returned over 10 days, amalgamated to show a group verdict on each recommendation and presented to the group meeting seven days later. The comments are available (without attribution) to help focus discussion. As would be expected, about 75% of decisions have a clearly demonstrated consensus and require no further discussion. The rest are discussed and after amending the wording, the group can revote using real-time electronic keypads to confirm the change in opinion. About half the changes are clarifications of wording or removal of ambiguity. The remainder have needed re-examination of the evidence, issues or implications before redefining the recommendation. The process has been used in four guidelines and participants have been both compliant and complementary. Over 95% have done the home vote in time for the meeting and all have participated. Each subgroup (patients, doctors, other healthcare clinicians and guideline technicians) seems to have used the system with equal facility and participation. The first private vote allows individuals to make up their own minds and to check evidence or seek advice as required. Having knowledge of all opinions in advance enables the meeting to focus on issues of disagreement and show how each disagreement has been resolved.

National Collaborating Centre for Cancer

Service guidance being developed by the NCC for Cancer as part of the series 'Improving Outcomes in Cancer' has particular problems, because it concentrates more on the configuration of care than on individual interventions. As a result, there is likely to be less relevant research evidence and a greater need to rely on consensus developed in the guideline development group. The NCC has therefore recruited the help of a team from the University of Glamorgan to support the work of the guideline development groups (GDGs). The team will attend GDG meetings on a regular basis and, if the group is happy to use this support, they will monitor group process by observation and tape recording of either all or part of the meetings. Transcripts will be made of important interactions, which will be analysed and feedback will be provided as required. This information should provide insights into the decision-making processes and the development of ideas as well as aiding the achievement of consensus. In addition they will be able to provide group support through the occasional use of specially developed handsets and software.[2] These allow anonymised voting on specific, predetermined questions and the results to be displayed to the group as histograms. Discussion can then take place about the results of the votes without individuals having to declare their own voting preference. This can be useful in providing a 'safer' environment for the discussion. Further voting can take place if needed to see if the group opinion has shifted. The technology will be demonstrated to the group and they can decide whether and when they wish to use it. This may be particularly useful when a point is reached when consensus is proving difficult to achieve.

References

1   Murphy MK, Black NA, Lamping DL *et al.* (1998) Consensus development methods, and their use in clinical guideline development. *Health Technology Assessment* **2 (3)**.

2   Groves S, Gear T, Prince J and Read M (2002) *Dialogue in Practice: a methodological approach to modelling group processes with on-line support.* Proceedings: Developing Philosophy of Management Conference, Oxford.

What approaches have been used in assessing new interventional procedures? A clinician's view

Trevor Cleveland

Interventional procedures, in the healthcare environment, are generally taken to include most surgical operations and the so-called 'minimally invasive' procedures, that have been developed to reduce the morbidity and mortality of such operations. Drugs and other pharmacological interventions are usually regarded separately. There are very few examples of genuinely new interventions, the majority of new procedures are modifications of established procedures, or technological changes that enable a similar alteration to be effected, but without the need for an open surgical operation.

The difficulty presented by such developments is to identify if the changes proposed really do translate into a benefit. To make the situation more complex, benefit can be regarded in a number of ways:

- improved effectiveness of the procedure, such as a more durable operation
- reduced mortality
- reduced morbidity
- improved recovery period
- improved patient acceptability
- reduced cost (direct costs are often increased, but there may be benefit in terms of less use of healthcare resources in the long term and less time lost from employment, etc.)
- increased range of patients for whom treatment is possible.

Many of the developments in the interventional arena centre around the push towards less invasive procedures, with less time needed for patient recovery and less need for in-hospital patient care. The impetus for such developments has been provided by all groups involved: patients generally prefer to have as short an inpatient hospital episode as possible, doctors prefer to treat patients in as uncomplicated a fashion as possible and the healthcare providers see benefit in such developments. In addition, the technological advances that engineering allows, result in a rapid and innovative change in the technologies that are available.

There are a number of examples of such changes that have received widespread publicity (in the medical and lay press, along with the television, radio and the Internet), and indeed have become the standard care. Such examples include coronary angioplasty and stenting replacing bypass grafting, laparoscopic cholecystectomy and extracorporal shock wave lithotripsy for kidney stones. Historically, advances in operative techniques have been introduced in the expectation that benefit would be gained. The present culture of collecting evidence for new procedures prior to their introduction, whilst laudable, would probably have delayed the introduction of these techniques. On the other hand, some of the mistakes made during such introduction would have been avoided.

The medical literature contains information that can be graded in terms of the degree of reliance that may be placed on those data. Level 1 data (the best) relies on the conduction and completion of randomised trials of techniques and the meta-analysis of case controlled series. This grading system stretches to level 4 data, which relies on the opinion of experts. However, even when there are level 1 data for a procedure, considerable doubt and controversy may still exist. For example the first carotid endarterectomy was performed in the 1950s, but level 1 data on this procedure (as provided by large trials in both Europe and the USA) were not available until the 1990s. Even then controversy remains, and in addition there is doubt as to whether such data are applicable to the practice of today. Thus some 40 years elapsed, during which a great number of people were thought to have benefited from the procedure and large costs were incurred in generating such data, but still the situation is in doubt. In addition, during this time considerable public interest brought significant pressure to bear on the medical community to perform the procedure, so that this became the most commonly performed vascular surgical procedure in the USA in the 1980s.

In order that the potential situation of denying patients the perceived benefits of a new procedure does not occur, a more rapid method of introduction of new procedures needs to be found. However, such a method requires that the procedure does indeed accrue benefit, and is not causing harm. It is assumed that all new procedures are developed with the intention of improving patients' well-being. However, there may be a risk that has not been appreciated. Often a new concept is put into practice for the benefit of a patient or group of patients who seem to have little alternative. A successful outcome then is communicated with other medical practitioners through the scientific literature or medical conferences. Following such peer review, the technique may be adopted by other practitioners, and so a move to use the procedure gathers momentum. At some stage along the line this receives publicity in the lay press and further enthusiasm results.

Once a new procedure begins to gain some popularity the question arises as to how frequently it is being performed, for what indications is it being used and what success (or otherwise) is being achieved. At such a point there are usually calls for formal trials, which may well be ideal. However, the funding for such trials may be difficult and the sums required large. In the meantime what should be done for those patients who may benefit from the new procedure, and who may be asking for it? One way to address this is to form a registry of practice, either nationally or internationally.

Setting up such a registry is much cheaper than a randomised trial, but is scientifically less sound. However, it can be established much more quickly and may act as a pilot for future studies. There are problems with starting up a national registry including:

- who funds it
- who runs it
- data entry is voluntary, and may therefore be incomplete
- validation of the data once collected
- patient consent
- data protection
- dissemination of the results.

However, despite such limitations, registry data may be very useful in monitoring and auditing new procedures. The data generated may subsequently be useful in planning more formal studies, or assessing the need to provide services. The issues of forming such a registry will be discussed during the NICE conference.

The role of patients and the public in generating research evidence

Sarah Buckland

Introduction

The active involvement of the public in research can help to improve the quality of the evidence base from which decisions about healthcare are made. Public involvement helps to ensure that research is relevant and acceptable to those who use health and social care services. Health research that is carried out without public involvement risks avoiding issues that are of importance to the end users of services, for whom health research is ultimately aiming to benefit. This paper draws on some work carried out by INVOLVE, to illustrate the contribution the public can make to the development of research evidence. INVOLVE (formerly Consumers in NHS Research) is funded by the Department of Health, and has a national remit to promote and support the active involvement of the public in research in order to improve the way that research is prioritised, commissioned, undertaken, communicated and used.

Discussion

The term 'public' is used here to describe patients, and potential patients, informal (unpaid) carers, users of health and social care services, disabled people and representatives of people who use services, as well as those who are the potential recipients of public health programmes and social services interventions. Active involvement of the public in research is about doing research 'with' or 'by' the public rather than 'to', 'about' or 'for' the public, where the people who use services are active partners in the research process, rather than just the 'subjects' of research. Members of the public have been involved in research for many years and in many different ways. This can range from advising on research priorities and research design through to planning and undertaking the research themselves.

Controlled trials have traditionally been designed and carried out by clinicians and academics, with the only role of patients or the public being as the 'subjects' of the research. However, attitudes and approaches are changing and there is a growing acceptance of the contribution that members of the public are able to make as active participants in the research process. It is essential that the public are involved in trials, as the priorities and concerns of people who use services are not always the same as those of clinicians and academics.[1]

Some of the main ways that the public have been involved in trials have been through participation on steering groups and advisory groups, in the design of patient information materials and in the dissemination of research.[2] However, they can be involved in all stages of the research.

The following are examples of the ways that the public have influenced the design and execution of trials. These are taken from interviews with researchers and members of the public who were involved in a small number of randomised controlled trials, where the public were actively involved in the trials.[3]

Improving the relevance of controlled trials

Public involvement improved the relevance of the trials by highlighting issues of importance to the public, challenging the assumptions of the researchers and identifying additional outcome measures which reflected the concerns of potential service users.

Members of the public were involved in the design and execution of trials of hormone replacement therapy (HRT) for those with a history of early-stage breast cancer. They participated in initial discussions as well as subsequent workshops to prioritise the action points to be incorporated into the national study. These resulted in the decision that the trials should include the use of alternative therapies as well as HRT. In another trial to assess the effect on people's health of improving housing conditions, it was suggested by the residents that environmental outcomes should be considered alongside health outcomes.

Improving the acceptability of trials

The public also had a vital role to play in improving the acceptability of trials, by advising on the methods proposed and by improving the quality of information provided to participants. For example, they advised on issues such as the sensitivity of the wording of patient information; whether information was either too complex or patronising; the timing of interventions; the acceptability of proposed methods such as the use of placebos; and the need for support to participants in the trials.

Public involvement can assist in improving the recruitment to trials as well as the retention of participants on trials. Advice from the public on the value of keeping participants and the wider community informed of the progress and importance of trials was felt to have contributed to the success of the trials. For example, in a trial to improve housing conditions the tenants involved encouraged participation in the study, and in another trial on the use of zidovudine (AZT) in symptom-free HIV infection, it was felt that such involvement helped to ensure that research participants continued with the trial.

Research that is more user friendly and acceptable to participants is likely to increase the chances of people agreeing to participate.

Conclusion

While there is, as yet, little scientific evidence to demonstrate the effectiveness of public involvement in improving the quality of research, there is a strong ethical argument for involving the public as well as an increasing body of literature that illustrates the contribution that the public are making to research.[4,5]

References

1   Campbell R, Quilty B and Dieppe P (2003) Discrepancies between patients' assessments of outcome: qualitative study nested within a randomised controlled trial. *British Medical Journal* **326**: 252–3.

2   Hanley B, Truesdale A, King A, Elbourned D and Chalmers I (2001) Involving consumers in designing, conducting and interpreting randomised controlled trials: questionnaire survey. *British Medical Journal* **322**: 519–23.

3   Buckland S *et al.* (forthcoming report) *Involving the Public in RCTs: case studies from researcher and public perspectives*. INVOLVE: Eastleigh.

4   Boote J, Telford R and Cooper C (2002) Consumer involvement in health research: a review and research agenda. *Health Policy* **61** (2): 213–36.

5   Hanley B, Bradburn J and Barnes M (2004) *Involving the Public in NHS, Public Health and Social Care Research: Briefing notes for researchers* (2e). INVOLVE: Eastleigh.

MATCH: a role for academia and major research funders in generating research evidence

Terry Young

Scene setting

Two questions are worth asking about how the academic sector might support industrial players in major health markets:

- Why should academics be able to make a contribution to a sector where the environment, pressures and drivers are so different from their own?
- How can such research make a contribution to global markets worth many orders of magnitude more than the research investment?

Introduction to MATCH

The Multidisciplinary Assessment of Technology Centre for Health (MATCH) faces these questions as it commences its research aimed at the medical devices sector. MATCH is a five-year research collaboration by the Universities of Birmingham, Brunel, KCL, Nottingham and Ulster, funded by the Engineering and Physical Sciences Research Council (EPSRC), with other sponsors including the Department of Trade and Industry (DTI), Invest Northern Ireland and the National Patient Safety Agency. It is also supported by more than 20 industrial partners with cash and in-kind contributions that raise the investment to about £6.5 million. This is likely to rise with increasing industrial support.

Critical links

So why might academics be able to contribute? The key point here is to discover a link between intellectually compelling problems and industrially critical problems. If such a connection exists, then there is motivation for the academics and motivation for industry to want the involvement of academics. In MATCH, there are three such strands, and indeed, a research project has been built around each.

As the medical device sector comes under greater pressure to provide evidence of efficacy (alongside the traditional criterion of safety), it needs methods in effective, affordable trials. This connects into some Bayesian theory targeted at fusing knowledge of different types. Essentially, the more you know about a new medical product (and can show in a formal way that you know it), the less uncertainty there is to be resolved through trials. Ultimately, through appeal to simulation or other surrogates, methods may emerge to eliminate trials in some cases and greatly reduce their size, cost and duration in others. This project (Project 1) aims also to support the healthcare technologists with a common view of value that is shared by users, manufacturers, regulators and reimbursement agencies, developing and using new methods where appropriate. Figure A indicates how these projects fit into the academic/industrial spectrum.

Second, in the fragmented world of (often small) UK companies producing medical technology, there is constant pressure to find more affordable and effective manufacturing processes. This opens up a research agenda for a second project (Project 2) in methods for optimised processes, examining the decisions

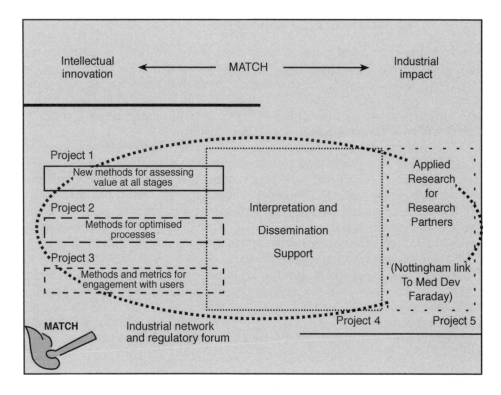

Figure A   A conceptual view of MATCH and the intellectual space it occupies.

around selection of concepts for development, through the process of manufacture and delivery.

Third, industry would significantly mitigate the risk of a product failing in the market if it could be sure that it fully understood the users' needs. The associated academic agenda (Project 3) is perhaps the most challenging of all in seeking to synthesise new methods to capture user needs, appealing to a broad spectrum of techniques in the social sciences, medicine and nursing, and reaching into engineering.

Academics can also contribute where there is space to work with industrialists. From the proposal onwards, MATCH has been firmly targeted at industry. Industrial staff came into the proposal-writing process and MATCH has projects dedicated both towards providing an industrial take on the research (Project 4) and a project in which academics and the industrial partners can jointly apply the new methods to real medical devices (Project 5). The aim of these initiatives is to ensure that the academic research is applied meaningfully as soon as possible, and also that, by applying the emergent methodologies to real products, the research will be enriched and remain focused on relevant industrial issues.

Punching above our weight

And so to the second key question: even if MATCH reaches £1 million per year, how could it affect a £100 billion annual global market? Here are two suggestions. First, this research is about changing things through ideas, so the quality of the concepts is critical. If MATCH cannot synthesise effective methods around device value (Project 1), optimised process (Project 2) or user needs (Project 3), then it will have failed, whatever the level of investment.

On the other hand, if the ideas are sound, they have the potential to nucleate a new debate with important communities. For instance, if the industrial community can be supported with better, more open, more auditable processes and an advanced concept of product value, with the strategies for demonstrating it, there should be scope for a proactive engagement with regulators and reimbursement agencies. To this end, MATCH aims to run a regulatory forum, fuelled with the findings of the research and engaging all stakeholders.

The final opportunity for a modest establishment such as MATCH to have an impact on the wider world is through leverage in all its networks. MATCH has courted the industrial community throughout and must now operate leverage within this network. The MATCH industrial partners have 5–7% of the market, and, by convincing these partners and growing the network, the ideas should percolate around the sector. Again, Figure A attempts to capture some of this thinking.

Summary

The rationale behind a piece of industrially relevant research is described in order to answer two critical questions. We believe that academics can contribute meaningfully across the academic/industrial divide in this case because there are several threads linking compelling research to a critical industrial agenda. Furthermore, we suggest that, while research funding is miniscule when compared to the market size, the networks exist through which high-quality ideas can be taken up by the industrial community itself and may also nucleate a new debate, particularly with respect to regulation and reimbursement.

PART THREE

Raising standards – national policy and practice

Social care and joint working with the NHS: how the Social Care Institute for Excellence works with NHS partners

Amanda Edwards and Patricia Kearney

Introduction

The Social Care Institute for Excellence's (SCIE's) corporate plan identifies that partnerships are essential to the success of its work, as it is only through others that SCIE's work will have an impact on the quality of services. The plan describes a number of ways in which SCIE will work with others:

- partnerships to develop a common product
- joint work where there is a common interest
- consultation to seek specialist expertise
- partnerships to promote participation
- work with representative organisations, the voluntary sector and other stakeholders
- developing synergy between SCIE and the training and regulatory bodies in the four jurisdictions
- the partners' council (where users, carers and other stakeholders influence SCIE's priorities, advise on its work programme and monitor its performance).

Such a variety suggests that a framework for understanding external relationships may be helpful and SCIE has made use of the one described below. It has been developed by Michael Fine and colleagues during the course of studies on co-ordination in community care.[1]

A framework for understanding joint working and partnership

Fine *et al* (1998) comment that given the widespread interest in improving co-ordination it is surprising how little published work there has been defining such frequently used concepts as co-ordination and integration.[1] They make a distinction between the voluntary commitment suggested by terms such as co-operation and the tighter, more directed actions implied in the word co-ordination. The latter, they argue, suggests adherence to a plan or protocols – some form of external control, which is not dependent solely on the goodwill of the participants. Fine's review of the literature finds that there is no single approach that can provide solutions to the problems of service fragmentation in community care. Instead he proposes that the concepts applied to different degrees of collaboration form a scale or continuum, which extends from autonomy to integration, to distinguish between the various types of activity across organisational boundaries.

- Autonomy is when the agencies act without reference to each other, although their actions may affect one another.
- Co-operation is when parties show a willingness to work together with an emphasis on communication.
- Co-ordination is when considerable effort is put into harmonising the activities of agencies so that duplication is minimised. It is often characterised by the activity of a third party to co-ordinate, and the existence of agreed protocols.
- Integration is when the boundaries begin to dissolve and new work units emerge.

Fine's framework shows the importance of distinguishing between the variety of arrangements that go under the broad heading of partnership. Most of SCIE's activities fall into the categories of co-operation or co-ordination (this may not be quite the right term to describe SCIE's activities in this category, but the features that Fine and colleagues apply to co-ordination are helpful).[1]

Putting the framework into practice

When putting these aspirations into practice it helps to remember some of the characteristics of organisational life. First, most institutions presume that their own world is universal and that all other organisations work in the same way. In moving from commitment to co-ordination, to use Fine's terms, SCIE and its fellow organisations have found that it helps to do some reciprocal preparation. This involves:

- being clear about what we do and why and how we do it
- not assuming prior knowledge about the other organisation

- finding out what the other does
- finding matters of common interest
- defining the aims of the partnership, which helps shape the methods by which these can be achieved
- seeing the differences: function, methods, vocabulary (not always all three) and therefore the similarities
- agreeing boundaries, differing remits and responsibilities.

This approach helps to diminish the usual concerns and preconceptions raised by joint working about where the power lies in the arrangement: is this collaboration, merger or takeover? The common understandings it creates clear the way for effective working together to achieve more than either organisation could do in isolation.

Some practical results

Examples of co-operation with other organisations include:

- work with the National Electronic Library for Health, particularly about electronic and web resources for people with learning disabilities
- work with a number of academic institutions with a shared interest in the development of systematic review, e.g. the Evidence for Policy and Practice Information (EPPI) Centre at the Institute of Education, with the Campbell Collaboration and internationally with the Swedish Centre.

We have already begun to develop partnerships with organisations with whom we have shared aims and interests. Such partnerships have tangible results such as SCIE's joint appointment with the National Institute for Mental Health in England (NIMHE) of two fellows in social care. SCIE's work with NICE provides a further example. We have drawn up a partnership agreement that will provide a framework for future joint work and relationships between SCIE and NICE. The agreement has already proved useful in providing a framework for some work we have done with NICE about palliative care guidelines, as a basis for work between NICE and SCIE on the NICE guidelines programme and in our joint work on the technology appraisal on the effectiveness of parent/ education programmes in the treatment of conduct disorders in children.

Reference

1   Fine M, Thomson C and Graham S (1998) *Evaluation of New South Wales Demonstration Projects in Integrated Community Care.* Social Policy Research Centre: University of New South Wales.

The impact of emergency care targets on the quality agenda

K George MM Alberti

At the inception of the NHS, casualty departments of acute hospitals were staffed by junior doctors wishing to broaden their experience. Medical and surgical emergencies were generally referred directly to the acute teams. Over the next two or three decades there was a slow move to a consultant-supervised system, but with the main emphasis on trauma rather than illness. Over the past decades there has been the emergence of emergency medicine as a major speciality with a shift to more medical conditions and major trauma becoming the province of specialised units. Despite this, emergency departments have been a low priority for investment, generally overcrowded, not well organised and with very long waiting times.

The NHS Plan, published in 2000, unequivocally stated that 90% of all people attending emergency departments should be dealt with and admitted or discharged within four hours.[1] This figure was due to rise to 100% by 2004. The immediate impact was the publication of *Reforming Emergency Care* in late 2002, which was a blueprint for action.[2]

So what has happened? First, the impact of the target has been to focus attention on emergency care as never before. The Emergency Care Collaborative was established to enable trusts first to examine their own performance, next to discuss ways of improving with others and then to implement changes. Performance increased dramatically between 2002 and the 31 March 2003 target date and has been sustained at around that level.

Two types of change have occurred. First, the alterations in systems and process are being implemented. This has come about through analysis of blocks in the system and also the contribution of different professionals to care. Second, physical changes in departments and improved staffing are occurring, although this is inevitably slower and requires substantial resources.

It has become apparent that patients were often being treated by inappropriate staff. The principle that a patient should be seen by an experienced professional capable of dealing with their problem immediately has greatly speeded up care. Emergency nurse practitioners have been created and carry much of the burden of so-called 'minors'. Skills and competence have become the criteria for 'who does what?' rather than post-nominal letters. On the physical side, the establishment of proper children's facilities, observation units and assessment units has greatly enhanced patient care and patient experience. Very long waits on trolleys are almost unknown as the flow through the system improves. At the same time, emergency care for certain categories of patients – such as those with myocardial infarction or stroke – has been enhanced with input from the appropriate National Service Frameworks (NSFs).

During these improvements it has become obvious that many of the problems of emergency care are outside the control of the emergency department. Thus, within the hospital, inadequate bed numbers and/or poor bed management can lead to back pressure on the emergency department. Rapid and effective action of the inpatient speciality teams can also greatly improve performance of the emergency department.

The other major area for change is the community. Effective links with social care both to prevent admission and to speed discharge are vital. The creation of a network of urgent care centres (walk-in centres and minor injury units) is beginning, with the emphasis on appropriate care closer to home. There is also the development of community teams for the elderly, those with mental health problems and for chronic disease management. Emergency care practitioners are also being developed from paramedics and nurses, with the intent to improve and enhance first-contact care. Organisationally emergency care networks are being developed in all areas to establish local needs, plan emergency services and integrate activities of all the organisations involved.

It is assumed that all these measures will take forward the quality agenda. Certainly there will be more choice for patients. Undoubtedly waiting shorter times for treatment must be beneficial. However, robust outcome measures are now needed to prove that clinical quality has improved in parallel with patient experience.

There has been a step change for the better in emergency care in the past two years – stimulated by the *NHS Plan* targets.[1] Much remains to be done, and at least another five years will be required, but much has already been achieved.

References

1   Department of Health (2000) *The NHS Plan: a plan for investment, a plan for reform.* Department of Health: London.

2   Department of Health (2002) *Reforming Emergency Care: achieving the* NHS Plan *targets.* Department of Health: London.

Progressive quality management: creating sustainable changes in professional practice

Jon Harvey

Quality management is simple. All you have to do is to ensure that every person and system in the NHS delivers services right the first time – where 'right' means the agreed requirements of the stakeholder now and in the future. Such requirements are various – depending on the stakeholder – but very broadly speaking for users/patients (and their families) this means providing a service that is tuned to their needs and wishes, is clinically effective (evidence based) and leads towards the person in question having years added to their life, and life added to their years.

However, despite earnest attempts to make such a simple approach happen, mistakes are often made ...

For example, in many organisations, the process can become too inward looking. Although there is much talk about the need for delighting the external customer, some organisations have fallen into the trap of consuming vast quantities of staff time and energies on designing intricate quality procedures and endless efforts to ensure that internal departments are aligned effectively with each other. The external client or stakeholder hardly gets a look in and is almost certainly only very cursorily involved in setting the (so-called) quality standards and procedures.

In some organisations there is inadequate investment in the foundations for success – both in design and implementation. Insufficient time is taken to plan how best to start, where to start and with whom. Moreover the staff involved are exhorted to provide a quality service, employ lots of new quality tools and techniques and become enlightened masters of the art of patient or customer care without adequate training, facilities or time.

Another common feature of unsuccessful quality strategies is fragmented and inconsistent policy and decision making. Although there is often lots of rhetoric about 'people being our most important asset' and 'quality is all we are in business to do', there often remain explicit policies on (for example) equal opportunities, health and safety, training and development, complaint handling, community engagement, clinical governance, etc, which are at best uncoordinated and at worst in opposition to each other. When these polices are then mixed with the raft of implicit 'accepted' practices on promotion, budget building or strategy formation (for example), the eventual result can be a confusing fragmented mush or battle zone within which no quality strategy has a hope of succeeding.

Without a doubt, one of the most powerful inhibitors of developing and then implementing an effective quality strategy is insufficient commitment and 'role modelling' from senior leaders – which includes senior staff, non-executives, middle managers and trade union officials. Quality management requires a palpable commitment to continuous improvement and frontline empowerment (among other key ingredients). These principles in turn require leaders to be committed to and capable of reflection, learning and change, a willingness to share power and authority where it is in the interests of the patients and other key stakeholders, and a giving up of any attachment to a management style based on bullying, fear and lack of respect. These are major challenges to many leaders – who have perhaps gained their position on precisely the opposite qualities. But the lessons are clear – superlative performance only comes from organisations where managers and leaders are actively pursuing such principles.

When attempts are made to change the culture of organisations (as quality management strategies seek to do), a great deal of resources are invested in 'pushing the boat out' as it were – communicating the messages, training people in new skills, introducing new procedures to support the activity and so forth. However, it is well established that positive progress will not be made unless critical restraining factors (from within the structure, the culture or the procedures and practices which are working against quality objectives) are dealt with.

When public organisations embark on a quality management strategy, the initial focus for the efforts may well be on achieving an award (such as Investors in People) or developing an approach that is moulded around a model such as the European Quality Management Foundation Excellence Model. Such approaches can lead to 'fad fatigue' among the staff (who have 'seen it all before') or such a belief in the award or model ('awardmania'/'model myopia') that it becomes the goal rather than the vehicle for getting there.

Crucially it is in organisations which demonstrate an unwillingness to learn from the past that the most mistakes are made and the least progress with quality management is achieved.

What we need are approaches to quality management that are progressive and evidence based. Mindful that there are no 'wonder formulae' for delivering a successful progressive approach to quality management there are a number of building blocks that provide a useful foundation. These building blocks include:

- clear and agreed goals for health outcomes – to ensure common understanding and coherent efforts
- all leaders of the trust being actively engaged in being challenged and challenging each other to deliver inspirational leadership
- an overarching and integrating plan to drive forward on quality – and ensure there are no inconsistencies
- an integrated and multi-agency community engagement strategy – so that partner agencies and the public work with the NHS to generate health outcomes
- clear and agreed definitions of key terms: modernisation, quality, stakeholders, engagement and so forth
- a structure and resources to plan, manage and monitor the process
- an integrated communication and education strategy – to ensure the messages get through and staff are equipped to deliver quality
- the targeted use of continuous improvement tools, techniques and systems – less is often more
- a strategy for audit, evaluation and review – to ensure the overall process is evidence based
- a congruent performance management strategy – to focus everyone's efforts and value staff who go the 'extra mile'
- a dedicated plan to identify and tackle the restraining forces – be they structural, procedural or cultural.

Confidential Enquiry into Maternal and Child Health

Richard Congdon

Introduction

The Confidential Enquiry into Maternal and Child Health (CEMACH) was formed in April 2003 as part of the strategy for the national confidential enquiries of NICE. While CEMACH is a self-governing body, it is predominantly funded by NICE. CEMACH has taken over the enquiries into deaths of mothers, infants and stillbirths previously carried out by the Confidential Enquiry into Maternal Deaths (CEMD) and the Confidential Enquiry into Stillbirths and Deaths in Infancy (CESDI). CEMACH will be setting up an enquiry into child health and extending its range to include morbidity as well as mortality. The new enquiry's aim is to improve clinical outcomes for mothers, babies and children.

Elements of continuity

CEMACH will continue to fully respect the confidentiality not only of the patients involved in the cases it reviews, but also of clinicians and hospitals. CEMACH is about learning, not blaming. The enquiry will be strongly rooted in the professions whose work it evaluates. Its independent board includes representatives from the six Royal Colleges most closely associated with its work. CEMACH will continue to involve practising clinicians from across the country in its multidisciplinary enquiry panels.

Developing the programme

The enquiry's work falls into three distinct areas:

- mothers (to one year after delivery)
- perinatal (to 28 days)
- children (28 days to 16 years).

The CEMACH programme will provide a balanced coverage of all three groups. Naturally, wherever possible we will achieve synergies by designing projects to cover more than one of the above groups.

We will be developing the enquiry methodology to enhance its scientific robustness. CEMACH will use a variety of tools to achieve its objectives. Projects are likely to include case control studies as well as structured questionnaires, cohort analyses and clinical audits.

We will be actively seeking partners to enable joint projects to be undertaken. These partners may include other national confidential enquiries or research bodies, whose expertise may be valuable in deriving the maximum value from the data collected by the enquiry.

CEMACH is also keen to extend the participation of 'expert patients' and representatives of the many voluntary sector and charitable bodies involved in its areas of work.

Links to NICE Clinical Guidelines Programme

We will be seeking to align our work more closely with the NICE Clinical Guidelines Programme. The enquiry is well placed to ascertain whether practising clinicians are aware of NICE guidelines and are following them. In case control studies, CEMACH may be able to assess whether adherence to the published guideline is affecting outcomes for patients. The enquiry's work could also suggest new areas where guidelines are required or where amendments may be needed to existing guidelines.

Current programmes

CEMACH is currently involved in five strands of work:

- enquiry into maternal deaths
- data collection on perinatal mortality
- diabetes in pregnancy
- project 27/28
- child health.

Maternal enquiry

A triennial report is produced on every maternal death. In 2004 CEMACH will be reviewing the way ahead for the maternal enquiry. While it is expected that there will continue to be an important cyclical element, we will be exploring the scope to maximise the enquiry's impact by undertaking in-depth projects looking into both mortality and morbidity. Joint projects with other national enquiries or research bodies could prove particularly valuable in maternal health.

Perinatal mortality data

CEMACH runs a system for the collection of perinatal mortality data, the 'rapid report form'. We will be collecting data on losses from 22 weeks' gestation to 28 days old. We will be developing ways of feeding back trends and comparative data on mortality rates to trusts. This will include data to enable trusts to compare their own rates over time and, where there is agreement from the other trusts, with other hospitals in their region and in other regions. We will work with the Office for National Statistics (ONS) to achieve the minimum possible duplication of effort in the gathering and dissemination of these data.

Diabetes in pregnancy

CEMACH is currently undertaking a major project into diabetes in pregnancy based on an 18-month data set of diabetic pregnancies between March 2002 and October 2003. Emerging findings indicate that rates of perinatal mortality and congenital anomaly remain significantly higher for diabetic pregnancies than among the general population. The principal aim of the study is to examine the epidemiological, organisational and clinical factors that may be contributing to this situation and to make recommendations to improve outcomes.

The main reports expected will cover:

- the organisation of services for diabetic pregnancy (due shortly)
- the cohort of all diabetic pregnancies in the period under study
- the enquiry itself, which will include a case control study on periconceptional care and a clinical audit of care provided during pregnancy
- a proposal for a qualitative research project examining the care and advice services provided before and shortly after conception.

Project 27/28

Project 27/28 was a study of the impact of standards of clinical care on outcomes for babies born at 27 to 28 weeks' gestation. The report was launched by CESDI in March 2003, but there was no time for CESDI to undertake dissemination of this project prior to its dissolution. The new enquiry will seek to increase the dissemination of this project's findings. This will include the development of a clinical governance package for trusts.

Child health

CEMACH is committed to the development of a new national confidential enquiry into child health. It is, as yet, early days. Professional advisory machinery is currently being established for this new area of work. Proposals for possible areas of study and appropriate methodologies are expected in 2004.

Summary

CEMACH aims to absorb the work programmes it has inherited from CESDI and CEMD while developing the enquiry methodology and beginning new strands of work. The study of diabetes in pregnancy will represent the major commitment for CEMACH over the next two years. During that time, we will be preparing the new child health enquiry and developing an integrated forward programme of studies covering maternal, perinatal and child health.

The National Confidential Inquiry into Suicide and Homicide by People with Mental Illness: recent findings and new directions

Nicola Swinson and Navneet Kapur

Introduction

Suicide prevention is a priority for health services in England and is a central component of government strategy on public health and mental health services in the NSF (1999).[1] Recommendations arising from the inquiry report *Safer Services* (2001) have been incorporated into the National Suicide Prevention Strategy for England (2002).[2,3]

The National Confidential Inquiry into Suicide and Homicide by People with Mental Illness is a national clinical survey and aims to collect detailed clinical data on all suicides and homicides in people with contact with mental health services, and make specific recommendations on clinical practice and policy.

There are three stages to the data collection process for the suicide inquiry. First, a comprehensive national sample of all suicides, irrespective of psychiatric history, is collected. Second, individuals are identified who have been in contact with mental health services in the year before death. The third stage involves obtaining details of clinical care from the responsible consultant psychiatrist and his or her clinical team.

A parallel system of data collection operates for the homicide inquiry. Psychiatric reports and records of all previous offences are sought on all convicted homicides regardless of contact with services. The inquiry then proceeds as in the suicides inquiry and obtains clinical data on individuals with prior contact with mental health services *at any time.*

Recent findings

Suicide inquiry

The inquiry has been notified of 36 683 suicides in the general population since 1996, giving an annual rate of 10 per 100 000. Of these, 24% (8883) were in contact with mental health services in the 12 months before death. The inquiry currently holds data on 8446 suicides (97.3% response rate).

Because of our large sample size, it is now possible to carry out detailed subgroup analysis in order to inform specific suicide prevention strategies in different groups of patients.

Analysis of different age groups showed that older (> 75 years) suicides were less likely to have had contact with mental health services. Other significant differences are shown in Table A.

The distribution of primary diagnoses is shown in Figure A.

Inpatients constituted 16% of the inquiry sample. The predominant methods used were hanging or jumping, either from a height or in front of a moving vehicle. The majority had severe mental illness with high levels of co-morbidity, deliberate self-harm and isolation. Most suicides on the ward occurred by hanging, and structural barriers to observation were highlighted as a problem.

The most striking finding regarding suicides within three months of discharge from psychiatric inpatient care was the high level of suicide within the first two weeks (one-third). Forty per cent occurred prior to the first contact in the community. The individuals concerned also tended to have a more disrupted pattern of care, with several recent admissions and high levels of co-morbidity, substance abuse, violence, self-discharge and disengagement from services.

Table A   Suicide method used and characteristics of different age groups

	Young	Older
Method	Hanging and overdose	Hanging and overdose
	Jumping – height/moving vehicle	Drowning
Characteristics	Psychosis, personality disorder	Depression
	Substance abuse	Physical illness
	Recent loss of contact with services	Recent bereavement
	Unemployed	Isolation
		Suicide pacts (2%)

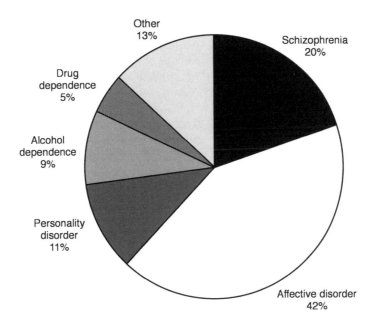

Figure A   Distribution of primary diagnoses in the suicide inquiry.

Homicide inquiry

The inquiry has been notified of 3645 homicides in the general population since 1996. Of these, 15% (559) are inquiry cases and the inquiry currently holds data on 491 homicides. Recent analyses have revealed that 34% of perpetrators had a lifetime history of mental disorder, yet less than one-fifth (18%) had ever had contact with mental health services and only 9% had contact in the preceding year; 15% had symptoms of mental illness at the time of the offence.

Substance misuse was diagnosed in over half of cases and alcohol or drugs contributed to 45% of all homicides; 22% of homicides were committed by people unknown to their victims. Rates of mental illness were lower, with alcohol and drugs more likely to be involved in the offence, compared with homicides where the victim was known.

New directions

Forty per cent of the suicide inquiry sample were psychiatric inpatients or had been recently discharged from inpatient care. They clearly constitute a high-risk group who are in close proximity to care and therefore might be amenable to interventions. This has led to the development of two case control studies of 250 inpatients and 250 post-discharge patients. These aim to compare clinical and social risk factors and identify differences in clinical care such as levels of supervision and compliance between suicides and controls. This will lead to the formulation of models of suicide and subsequent clinical risk assessment tools.

The inquiry is also expanding its data collection to include quantitative and qualitative information from primary care, emergency departments and relatives, using the psychological autopsy methodology. This has been an accepted method of characterising mental and psychosocial features of suicide victims for many years. However, given the sample size (200–250), analysis of subgroups will also be possible. This study aims to establish details of contact with primary care and emergency departments in the preceding 12 months, along with social and clinical circumstances and life events. Social and clinical antecedents of completed suicide, both generally and in specific subgroups, will be generated. The inquiry is also seeking to examine the feasibility of applying the psychological autopsy to homicide, by using similar methods of data collection and, in addition, supplementing this with information from perpetrators.

Other ongoing studies in which the inquiry is currently involved include investigating the relationship between service configuration and suicide rates, examining suicide rates and clinical and social predictors of completed suicide after episodes of deliberate self harm, and temporal monitoring of suicide rates. The inquiry has also recently taken over the management of the sudden unexplained death study. This is a national study which aims to monitor the number of sudden deaths in psychiatric inpatients and to carry out case control studies in order to examine the specific antecedents of sudden death.

A further expansion of the homicide study involves an examination of a national sample of people convicted for serious violence. Specifically, this study aims to examine rates of mental disorder and contact with mental health services and, subsequently, social and clinical characteristics of those with a history of contact with services who have committed serious offences.

References

1   Department of Health (1999) *National Service Framework for Mental Health*. DoH: London.

2   Appleby L, Shaw J, Sherratt J *et al.* (2001) *Safety First: Five-Year Report of the National Confidential Inquiry into Suicide and Homicide by People with Mental Illness*. DoH: London.

3   Department of Health (2002) *National Suicide Prevention Strategy for England*. DoH: London.

Raising standards in primary care

David Colin-Thomé

When general practitioners (GPs) voted overwhelmingly in June 2003 to accept the new General Medical Services (GMS) contract, we entered a new era of possibilities and opportunities to raise standards and radically transform the patient experience in the most utilised part of the NHS – primary care.

The GMS contract brings with it significant new funding and flexibilities for practices to develop their services for patients. And, for the first time in any health system, the new contract will establish systematic resourcing of practices on the basis of how well patients are cared for, not how many are treated.

This is a major shift. Traditionally, less than 4% of total spending on GP fees and allowances has been allocated to rewarding high standards. Now as much as a third of the resources practices receive will depend on meeting evidence-based quality standards set out in the new Quality and Outcomes Framework.

Within the framework, the clinical focus is on promoting and rewarding excellence in chronic disease management (CDM). This is certainly a radical move, but sharply rising global figures for chronic disease and the inevitability that this will be *the* health issue of the 21st century are facts demanding a robust response:

- in England alone almost nine million people live with chronic disease
- 40% of these have more than one condition
- chronic disease accounts for 80% of GP consultations and is a factor in 60% of hospital admissions
- the World Health Organization (WHO) is predicting that by 2020 chronic disease will be the largest global cause of disability.

The implications of these trends are huge for primary care where 90% of all patient journeys begin and end. Extra funding and clearer incentives to develop high quality and responsive services for chronic disease management are essential and GMS will give us these.

Of course the new contract by itself cannot deliver the improved outcomes we need for chronic disease sufferers. It will need to work hand-in-hand with the growing body of national standards and evidence-based support which the NSFs and NICE are now offering the NHS.

In meeting these standards, however, primary care trusts (PCTs) and practices need tailored and practical support at local level. One of the most successful programmes has been the National Primary Care Development Team's (NPDT) Primary Care Collaborative. With more than 3500 practices now engaged, the collaborative gathers and shares best practice, helping PCTs to systematically improve services.

The approach has yielded some groundbreaking results for patients with chronic conditions. Already, participating practices have achieved a four-fold reduction in mortality rates for patients with ischaemic heart disease. The NPDT is spreading that work throughout the wider NHS and is now looking at a similar approach for diabetics and patients with chronic lung disease.

While raising standards throughout primary care has to be about better care and improved health outcomes, the NHS vision is also about faster and more convenient access to care. By 2004, all patients will be able to see a GP within two working days or another primary care professional within one working day. The government has also said that at least one million more outpatient appointments should take place in primary care settings rather than hospitals by 2006.

These are tough challenges but we know they are achievable. There has been enormous progress on improving access in the past year – now nine out of ten people can get to see their GP within two working days. Again, the NPDT's collaborative approach continues to be one of the key supports. By July 2003, practices using the team's 'advanced access' model were seeing up to 70% reduction in waiting times to see a GP.

Enhancing the roles of highly skilled nurses and other primary care professionals is one of the central strands of advanced access. In fact it is fundamental to transforming standards in primary care and the wider NHS.

One of the exciting facets of GMS is that it is a practice-based contract – recognising that in delivering improvements and redesigning services round the needs of their local communities, PCTs and practices will need to make maximum use of the skills and potential of the whole primary care team. Improving access is one huge benefit, but the sort of multiprofessional services and integrated care emerging from these new ways of working are also crucial in enhancing pathways and supporting self-care for patients with chronic disease.

- Thousands of GPs, nurses, therapists and other professionals with a special interest (PwSIs) are utilising their specialist expertise in areas such as heart disease, diabetes and orthopaedics. They are bringing down waiting times and giving patients quicker, easier access to the range of care they need, including services that were once the sole domain of hospitals.
- *Liberating the Talents* was published last year to give practical support and strategic direction to PCTs to help unlock the potential of their nursing workforce.[1]

- More nurses and pharmacists are being trained as independent and supplementary prescribers and recommendations for a significant expansion of independent nurse prescribing are now with ministers.
- Locally based contracts for GPs (through the Personal Medical Services (PMS) contract), as well as new contracts for community pharmacists and dentists will support stronger partnerships and more innovative ways of delivering services in the community.

Avedis Donabedian, an American healthcare quality expert, maintained that quality is dependent on structure, process and outcomes. The NSFs, together with the new contract and fundamental changes in the funding and commissioning architecture of the NHS, are leading to better alignment than ever before between structure and process in the health service, which being evidence based will lead to better patient outcomes. PCTs – in control of 75% of the NHS budget – are in a powerful position as lead commissioners, and the new system of 'payment by results' will give them real teeth to drive up standards and put resources where they best serve patients.

If we are to raise standards for patients, we will of course need to listen to them and value their role as partners in their own healthcare. Already the Expert Patient Programme is training thousands of patients to help fellow sufferers manage their long-term conditions. In addition, the increasing numbers of nurse-led services and the potential of the proposed community pharmacy contract is putting a new emphasis on patient education and self-care.

The current national consultation on choice, responsiveness and equity will also set new directions for us in primary care. The landscape in primary care may be changing rapidly, but the organisations and individuals within it are more empowered than ever before to make real and sustainable improvements for patients.

Reference

1   Department of Health (2002) *Liberating the Talents*. DoH: London. www.doh.gov.uk/cno/liberatingtalents.htm

Further reading

- For more information on the new GMS contract see: www.doh.gov.uk/gmscontract/index.htm
- National Service Frameworks: www.doh.gov.uk/nsf/index.htm
- Reforming the NHS financial flows – introducing payment by results (The Department of Health October 2002): www.doh.gov.uk/nhsfinancialreforms/financialflowsoct02.pdf

- For an introduction to PwSIs and case studies see: www.doh.gov.uk/pricare/gp-special interests/servicestopatients.pdf
- The National Primary Care Development Team: www.npdt.org/scripts/default.asp?site_id=1
- The National Primary and Care Trust Development Programme (NatPaCT): www.natpact.nhs.uk/
- The Expert Patient Programme: www.doh.gov.uk/cmo/progress/expertpatient/index.htm

Measuring clinical performance

Jake Arnold-Forster

Governments boast of increased investment in healthcare. 'Thousands of new doctors and nurses recruited every year', 'New investment in technology and treatments' – those kinds of headline.

Yet the question for patients, voters, policy makers and healthcare workers is whether all this money is improving access to, and more importantly the quality of, healthcare. Despite the headlines, policy makers – including politicians – and the public want to see hard objective evidence that things are getting better, and that means some form of performance measurement. The arguments in favour of recording measures of performance – and publicising some of them – are familiar but controversial:

- information about how our public services are run should be given to citizens as a right not a benefit, remembering of course that citizens, patients and families of those patients are interested in different measures at different moments
- outcome measures are necessary to monitor performance in a system that is not regulated by the commercial market. Patients may still not have much choice, but that does not mean they should not know about the relative performance of their GP or hospital. It is the pressure that patients bring to bear using this information that exasperates clinicians, when it is used inexpertly, and improves performance when understood and used well
- the policy of extending choice to patients requires that they and their families have the right information to make those choices
- performance indicators provide a demonstration of improvements that managers and clinicians may feel are apparent, but citizens do not believe
- they are a vital mechanism for setting targets and driving improvements within an organisation. They can be both an incentive for improvement and a means of identifying areas for increased resources or attention
- they create a better understanding across the various groups within the healthcare system – doctors, nurses, managers and civil servants – about the relative priorities of the Secretary of State. This is especially important in a system which has a number of very important people (consultants, chief executives, Czars, etc) with no obvious chain of command but a very obvious overall boss.

Yet the drawbacks to performance indicators in healthcare are also well known and less controversial:

- they undermine patients' trust in doctors and the institutions they serve
- they are a distraction for clinicians from the main task of caring for people
- they create perverse incentives. For example, doctors complain that cutting waits for chronic but not dangerous conditions can distract them from cases where timeliness could make a difference
- they create a reason to cheat. As more managerial emphasis – and now financial reward – is based on these measures so the temptation to 'game' the system has become irresistible for some institutions
- technical measures are not understood by, and may even confuse, most patients
- the complexity of the processes involved in healthcare makes it impossible to construct the right balance between too many and too few of these indicators.

Whatever the merits of the arguments, the pros are winning and the cons losing. Star ratings, adverse incident reporting, mortality ratios, GP and consultant contracts, choice of hospital for elective surgery, the establishment of the Commission for Healthcare Audit and Inspection (CHAI) and, of course NICE itself, are all reflections of a desire to provide the NHS and the public with ways of judging healthcare.

So how should we measure the NHS? The great mass of networks and organisations that deliver, regulate and comment on the NHS appears to be coming to a consensus.

There should be a distinction between what should be measured nationally and what should be measured locally, although one set of data should not contradict the other. National measures should be as few and clear as possible. The same distinction should be applied to what should be made available to the general public, what should be open to patients (or their families) and what should be monitored internally. People who are judged, or feel themselves to be judged, by targets should feel they have control over which targets are used and whether the information defining them is accurately recorded. Doctors routinely complain, for example, that routinely collected data are inaccurate. The most obvious answer to this problem is to give those doctors a sense of ownership for any information that might be used to judge their effectiveness, by allowing them to see and audit it on a regular basis.

The creation of CHAI is adding new impetus to these debates in the UK. Internationally, WHO, the US-based Institute of Healthcare Improvement and others are seeking to try and answer some of these questions.

If the how has not been answered yet nor has the what. But again it is possible to detect an emerging consensus around the right national measures. *Access* is important because patients think it important. *Quality* of clinical care clearly matters to patients and clinicians. This phrase encompasses a range of indicators from redo rates for revascularisation to infection rates for specific hospital-borne bacteria. Naturally, *equity* of access and quality matters to the NHS because it was founded on that principle over 50 years ago. *Patient experience* of all of these measures is clearly important. Finally, the evident failure of the NHS to demonstrate *value for money* to the satisfaction of its political masters has also brought this measure out into the open.

The opportunity to create what the Centre for Health Information Quality has called 'a national information quality framework created locally and delivered personally' is now greater than ever. Policy now explicitly promotes providing timely and informative information to managers, clinicians and citizens. Huge amounts of money have been invested to make this happen.

Yet measuring the performance of the NHS will fail if it ignores the fundamental cultural and structural divisions within the UK health service. PCTs, acute hospital trusts, strategic health authorities (SHAs) and the Department of Health do not yet exchange information freely between themselves. There are noble exceptions, but managers and doctors do not tend to trust one another. One of the focuses for their lack of trust is performance measures. This has a simple history.

Broadly speaking, if Conservative governments created a quasi-market to better regulate efficiency in the NHS, Labour has listened to its focus groups and become obsessive about cutting waiting times. But this focus on access and efficiency has left many clinicians behind. The Hippocratic oath says nothing about timeliness or cost but obliges doctors to worry primarily about the quality of care for their patient.

If the government wants to engage doctors in managing the NHS they must create incentives for them to create and monitor measures of clinical quality. Equally, if doctors want to retain the trust of patients, they cannot hope that the demands to measure their performance will go away.

Four nations delivering a National Health Service

John Hill-Tout

Ways in which the four different nations of Britain can learn from each other about the delivery of healthcare: similarities and differences between systems, examples of working together and sharing best practice

In launching the strategic agenda of the Welsh Assembly Government, *Wales: a Better Country*, First Minister the Rt Hon Rhodri Morgan has said that 'with devolution, our destiny as regards health, wealth, education, the environment and the domestic agenda more widely, is increasingly in our own hands'. But it is equally acknowledged that while Wales has started the 21st century with new potential, it also faces some old challenges.

The Office for National Statistics reported that in 2001 the population of Wales stood at just over 2.9 million people, 44% of whom live in southeast Wales around Cardiff and the South Wales Valleys. Based on current trends, according to the Government Actuary's Department, the population is anticipated to rise to just over three million people by the year 2026. Like many countries, our population is growing older. In 2001, 17.4% of the population was aged 65 and over, and is expected to rise to 22.9% within the same time frame.

Wales has traditionally suffered high levels of poor health. For example, in the 2001 census, 12.5% of the population of Wales reported that their health was 'not good'. Merthyr Tydfil, an area of deprivation, had the highest percentage at 18.1% and Monmouthshire, where the level of deprivation is much lower, reported the lowest level of ill health at 9.5%. This was still above the average in England reported at 9%. To meet these old challenges, the Welsh Assembly Government has embarked on a radical programme of reform for the NHS in Wales. In April 2003, 22 local health boards replaced five health authorities and a newly combined Health and Social Care Department of the Government will now support these new NHS bodies.

In future, services will be more closely tailored to local needs and there will be greater focus on promoting better health, as well as delivering improved services. Policies will be more evidence based, backed by a robust financial strategy with greater freedom for success and stronger sanctions. Key Welsh health priorities include: improving access to primary, emergency and elective care; ensuring appropriate access to screening, immunisation and vaccination services; and improving the standard of care and delivery to specialist groups, such as coronary heart disease, cancer, diabetes, substance misuse and mental health. These objectives will be backed by more sophisticated workforce planning, improved technology and investment in the estate.

In Wales, it has been recognised that some services are best commissioned and sometimes delivered on a national basis. The newly formed Health Commission Wales, which is a unit of the Welsh Assembly, will be responsible for planning and commissioning specialised health services on an all-Wales basis. These will include specialist cancer care services, cardiac services and the Welsh Blood Service to name but a few.

From April 2004, subject to legislation, Healthcare Inspectorate Wales will be launched. A unit of the Welsh Assembly, it will undertake inspections of and investigations into the provision of healthcare on behalf of and by Welsh NHS bodies. To support this process, it is our intention to set up an advisory board for healthcare standards. This body will support the minister in the publication of a statement of standards, against which the performance of the NHS in Wales will be measured and maintained.

The Welsh Assembly Government recognises that citizens and communities will need to be involved in the decision making about health and social care services and must contribute by taking greater responsibility for their own health. It has, therefore, been decided to retain and strengthen the roles of community health councils. These independent bodies are able to bring an independent perspective to bear on complaints. They also have a unique blend of experienced officers and members who can provide effective support to complaints advocates in their dealings with the NHS.

The Welsh Assembly Government has structured the NHS in Wales to deliver services tailored to the needs of the population of Wales. Roles are being clarified and accountabilities strengthened with enhanced incentives, improved information and better performance management.

The Welsh Assembly Government will continue to target resources in the drive to remove barriers to early treatment and the promotion of ill health prevention.

New commitments include abolishing prescription charges to ensure people are not barred from treatment because of the cost of medicines. Primary school children in 'communities first' areas, which are those areas of Wales identified as most deprived, will receive free breakfasts from September 2004. The disabled will benefit from the scrapping of home care charges, which will ensure that they can afford the care needed to maintain as much independence as possible in their own homes.

The Welsh Assembly Government is committed to collaboration with the other UK nations and, to a large degree, we are all dependent on each other's expertise and experience. The development of the National Service Framework programme is a very good example of where Wales has benefited from work done in England.

Wales too has expertise to offer. Based on the expertise and professionalism of the staff at the Velindre NHS Trust and University of Wales College of Medicine, the Cancer National Collaborating Centre commissioned by NICE in Cardiff earlier this year provides us in Wales with an opportunity to contribute fully in the development of guidelines for the care and treatment of those patients with cancer across England and Wales.

The theme of this session is about the four nations delivering a National Health Service. It is about sharing our experiences and expertise, and the work undertaken on behalf of the four nations by the National Screening Committee is testimony to this underlying principle.

The work undertaken by the National Screening Committee, together with the Welsh Assembly Government's determination to develop services in primary care to reduce the burden on the secondary care sector, has made possible a national programme of diabetic retinopathy screening. Through its development, we have gained valuable experience, implementing the National Screening Committee recommendations on a national basis, and we are keen to share these experiences, and others, with nations across the UK and beyond.

Inspecting the private sector

Ros Gray

Independent healthcare providers probably contribute about £4 billion of private healthcare revenue in the UK. As such, Nuffield Hospitals is the third largest provider, with some 44 hospitals, a national health screening service and a care home for older people.

Even so, only approximately 14% of the population has access to independent healthcare, a figure that is set to grow exponentially following the government's initiatives with regard to independent sector treatment centres and the Patient Choice Initiative.

These two projects alone probably represent the biggest change to the provision of health services in the UK since the conception of the NHS. This move will liberalise the supply of healthcare from that NHS monopoly. The change will be in the face of a critically changing environment for independent healthcare providers.

The increased demand for independent healthcare also brings a challenge to the way that this service is delivered. However, regardless of the required new delivery mechanisms, this industry has become better regulated over the past two years or so.

The Care Standards Act 2000, brought the new independent sector regulator (the National Care Standards Commission – NCSC) and a new set of regulations and national minimum standards against which services are now measured. This move was not helped by the fact that the commission was abolished by the Secretary of State for Health just 19 days after it was created. Since that time the regulator has struggled to register, inspect and report on the quality of services under the span of its control.

Services new to regulation have remained elusive to the inspectorate, the NCSC finding itself with limited resources to inspect the caseload already established and transferred from the previous regime at health authority level. Not surprisingly, those new to regulation, including private doctors and the providers of intense pulsed light source treatment have not been knocking the door down to the commission's offices to be registered.

Equally, members of the NCSC inspectorate have had enough on their minds with being abolished, moving to one of two new organisations (the Commission for Social Care Inspection (CSCI) or CHAI) and the immense challenge of trying to make do and mend with an IT system that may or may not transfer with them to either of those new organisations and cannot yet deliver the complex demands of an intelligent reporting framework.

As the previous Director of Private and Voluntary Healthcare at the NCSC, I feel qualified to comment, having worked in healthcare for the past 25 years and in recent years predominantly in independent healthcare; I was seen as poacher turned gamekeeper when taking up the role of the regulator!

However, I have been amazed when returning to the provider world, how people have received me back 'to the fold' as if I have spent the past two years on some other planet!

So, to put the record straight, the regulator is made of flesh and blood like the rest of us and wants the same as most people who are involved in caring for patients receiving treatment: on behalf of patients, the assurance that health-care, wherever it is delivered is of a high enough standard; that when things go wrong lessons are learned to avoid repetition; that good practice is shared; and that all these aspects of the quality of healthcare are examined in a methodical way and appropriate action taken.

Of course the regulations and standards that direct the work of the regulator are not without problems, many were obviously written by committee (one wonders if some were in a room where the building was on fire!). The regulations will transfer to the new legislation and many have contributed to their proposed change over recent months.

And what of the new commission (CHAI)? It got off to a shaky start with no chief executive for some time and a chair who clearly knew his own mind and how he wanted the commission to look. At the time of writing, CHAI is light on vision, strategy and structure, although it has just recruited the top jobs. Sir Ian Kennedy has stated that any real change to the way things are done will not happen for two to three years. He wants a system that turns data into informa-tion that can improve patient care.

So how can a provider build relationships with the regulator to achieve a 'win–win' situation and meet the ultimate goal of the new regulator?

Delivering a report to the Chief Medical Officer (CMO) on the state of cosmetic surgery in London attempted to achieve just that. The general NCSC approach to measuring providers against the national minimum standards using a 1–4 scale does not work with complex independent healthcare acute provision. How can a score be allocated when there may be some 20–30 elements that make up that standard (e.g. decontamination)? How well is risk to patients identified using that scoring mechanism? I would suggest poorly.

Using the approach adopted for the controls assurance standards in the NHS, cosmetic surgery providers in London were asked to self-assess their perfor-mance against the regulations and standards. An inspection team visited the establishments to validate the self-assessment process.

The results were fascinating and the full report is available on the NCSC website (www.carestandards.org.uk). Interestingly, some of the providers that performed poorly against the standards had over-estimated their performance significantly.

Working with the regulator in an honest appraisal of current performance is, in my mind, the only way forward.

In the words of the Scout movement – be prepared!

- Know the regulations and standards against which you will be measured.
- If you are unsure about the meaning of any of the above, ask your lead inspector.
- Appraise your service against those regulations and standards – honestly.
- Have a clear action plan in place to improve your organisation's performance.
- Remember that the legal duty to do this sits with the registered manager and responsible individual of the organisation.
- Also remember that the regulator has powers to make you meet a regulatory requirement and is not afraid to use them.

Increasingly, patients and others seeking treatment options will look to the regulator and providers to tell them about the quality of healthcare services to enable them to make an informed choice. Be ahead of the game and rest assured that the quality of the service you provide can take any challenge or scrutiny – that makes for a very comfortable night's sleep!

The Task Force on Medicines Partnership: implementing concordance in medicine taking

Joanne Shaw and Geraldine Mynors

The Task Force on Medicines Partnership is a Department of Health-funded programme which aims to help patients to get the most out of medications by involving them as partners in prescribing decisions (including those decisions where an informed patient decides to decline the treatment offered) and supporting them in medicine taking where the decision is to accept treatment. The Task Force is a truly multidisciplinary collaboration of 25–30 members involving doctors, pharmacists, nurses, patients, the NHS, the pharmaceutical industry and academics, supported by the Medicines Partnership Centre, an executive team carrying out the programme of the Task Force. The Medicines Partnership was set up at the beginning of 2002 as part of the *Pharmacy in the Future* programme under *The NHS Plan*.

Prescribed medication remains by far the most common from of therapeutic intervention, and new and more effective medicines are constantly being introduced. Using medicines to best effect is therefore of critical importance in successfully managing many, if not most, conditions. In the past, most attention has been devoted to guiding treatment decisions rather than involving patients in these decisions and monitoring whether the medicines selected are actually taken as prescribed. However, until issues of medicine taking are addressed, as well as questions of what to prescribe, a significant proportion of drugs will be wasted and the potential therapeutic gain envisaged by NICE in drawing up many of its guidelines will not be realised.

Non-compliance with prescribed medication is an age-old problem, with as much of 50% of medicines for long-term conditions (a growing area of health-care provision) not taken as prescribed.[1] The most recent systematic review of compliance by McGavock and colleagues showed that most non-compliance is the result of conscious choices made by patients rather than simply 'forgetfulness'.[2] Since then, new and potentially more effective medicines have been launched that may be easier to take and have fewer side effects than their predecessors. It is therefore not unreasonable to suppose that overall compliance rates should have improved. However, a recent update commissioned by Medicines Partnership across 12 therapy areas showed that non-compliance remains a major barrier to patients obtaining the most benefit from medicines.[3]

Non-compliance represents a major deficit in healthcare, as represented by three main types of cost:

- to patients and families, in terms of increased morbidity and mortality which could be prevented
- to the NHS, in terms of wasted medicines at a time of increasing pressure on prescribing budgets, but more importantly in terms of unnecessary expenditure on preventable illness
- to society in terms of lost working days and productive life, as well as carer costs.

There are many reasons why patients fail to get the most from medication (*see* Figure A). Past approaches to improving the situation have focused on professional and practical issues (the top two categories).

In contrast, concordance describes a process of prescribing that recognises that patients are not the passive recipients of prescribing decisions, but have their own views about their condition and treatment. Numerous studies have shown that patients' beliefs and views about medicines are a key influence on

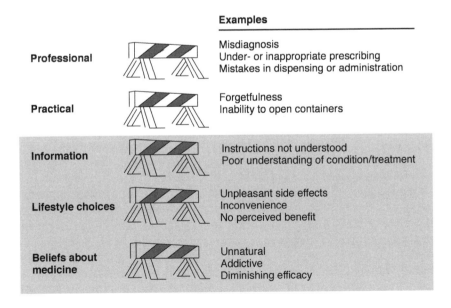

Examples

Professional
Misdiagnosis
Under- or inappropriate prescribing
Mistakes in dispensing or administration

Practical
Forgetfulness
Inability to open containers

Information
Instructions not understood
Poor understanding of condition/treatment

Lifestyle choices
Unpleasant side effects
Inconvenience
No perceived benefit

Beliefs about medicine
Unnatural
Addictive
Diminishing efficacy

Figure A Barriers to optimal use of medicine.

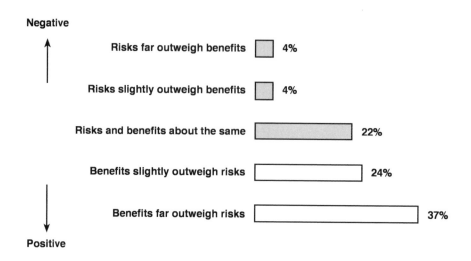

Figure B Public attitudes to medicines in general. *Source*: MORI survey of 2019 individuals, July 2003, available from Medicines Partnership.

whether and how they take them.[4] As many as 30% of patients (*see* Figure B) start with a basic belief that the benefits of medicines do not outweigh the risks or harms. Patients are much more likely to follow treatment if they have been active partners in prescribing decisions, and their views and preferences have been recognised and taken into account.[5,6]

This in turn is only possible if they have sufficient information and under-standing about the medicines available to them.[7]

Three elements need to characterise the health system if concordance is to be achieved (*see* Figure C).

In supporting the implementation of concordance, the Medicines Partnership has five areas of work.

1 *Professional development*: working to build concordance into the education and professional development of doctors, nurses and pharmacists to equip them with the attitudes, knowledge and skills to implement concordance in their professional practice. In addition, we are developing training tools and materials on shared decision making in medicines.
2 *Influencing patient and public expectations*: communicating with patients and the public to help them develop a better understanding of their medicines, and an expectation that they will be involved in prescribing decisions. In particular, during October 2003 we co-organised 'Ask About Medicines Week', a national campaign to encourage the public to be more proactive in finding out about their medicines. We also lead a consortium which is devel-oping and piloting medicines guides, a new structured source of information on medicines and treatment options, which will be available through NHS Online (and other channels over time).

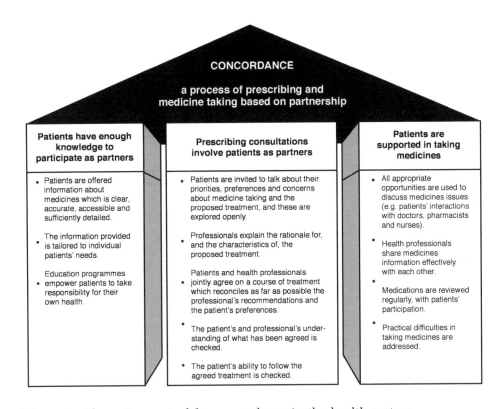

Figure C Elements required for concordance in the health system.

3 *Policy*: working with policy makers to ensure that patient partnership and concordance are embedded in the design and delivery of key policy initiatives. For example, we have produced guidance and practical tools on medication review to support the Older People's National Service Framework, which have been very widely taken up through the Medicines Partnership website.

4 *Research evidence*: drawing on the existing evidence base to identify strategies for putting concordance into practice and developing approaches to measure and audit results. Our research reports are available on our website.

5 *Model practice projects*: we are supporting 14 projects which demonstrate the potential for putting concordance into practice and producing measurable benefits within the NHS. In particular, we are supporting pilots to evaluate new forms of support for patients, such as nurse-led proactive telephone support, and the development of community pharmacists with special interests.

The potential to improve health outcomes through better use of medicines represents an enormous opportunity to the health system. Where patients are fully involved in prescribing decisions, they can be expected to be more compliant with the jointly agreed prescription. There is a need to recognise that many medicines are currently not taken, but that this fact is rarely discussed between health professionals and patients. Although some may find it hard to accept, a concordant approach may also identify those patients who, on an informed basis, choose to opt out of treatment, releasing NHS resources for other uses.

This work needs to concentrate on high-priority conditions and patient groups, fine tuning interventions that are most promising, with rigorous evaluation to establish what works and how it can be delivered cost-effectively for the benefit of patients.

References

1   Haynes RB, McDonald H, Garg AX and Montague P (2002) Interventions for helping patients to follow prescriptions for medications (Cochrane Review). *The Cochrane Library Issue 4, 2002*. Update Software: Oxford.

2   McGavock H, Britten N and Weinman J (1996) *A Review of the Literature on Drug Adherence*. Commissioned by the Royal Pharmaceutical Society of Great Britain as part of the project 'Partnership in Medicine Taking'. Royal Pharmaceutical Society: London.

3   Carter S, Taylor D and Levenson R (2003) *A Question of Choice: compliance in medicine taking* (2e). The Task Force on Medicines Partnership: London. www.medicines-partner ship.org/research-evidence

4   LaRosa JH and LaRosa JC (2000) Enhancing drug compliance in lipid-lowering treatment. *Archives of Family Medicine* 9: 1169–75.

5   Dayan-Lintzer M and Klein P (1999) Galenic, concerted choice and compliance with HRT. *Contraception, Fertilite, Sexualite* **27 (4)**: 318–21.

6   Cassileth BR, Zupkis RV, Sutton-Smith K and March V (1980) Information and participation preferences among cancer patients. *Annals of Internal Medicine* 92: 832–6.

7   Makoul G, Arntson P and Schofield T (1995) Health promotion in primary care: physician–patient communication and decision making about prescription medications. *Social Science and Medicine* **41 (9)**: 1241–54.

Partners for change? The impact of service user participation on change and improvement in social care services

Sarah Carr

This summary brings together the key themes and findings from the synthesis of six literature reviews on the impact of user participation on change and improvement in social care services. Reviews on older people, children and young people, people with learning difficulties and disabled people were commissioned by the Social Care Institute for Excellence (SCIE). Reviews on mental health service user participation and on general user/consumer involvement were commissioned by NHS Service Delivery and Organisation Research and Development (NHS SDO). The aim of this paper is to provide a brief, comprehensive account of what is known about this topic.

Messages for policy and practice

Efforts to involve people in the planning and development of the services they use are taking place across the UK. What remains unclear is the impact of that participation. At local and regional levels, policy makers would be advised to integrate change mapping and feedback into the whole participation process. Monitoring and evaluation techniques should be developed with service users.

Messages from research show the need for a range of models of involvement, depending on the level of activity to which participants wish to commit. What is important is that the choice is there, and that the involvement – or partnership – is real. User participation should relate clearly to a decision that the organisation plans to make, and is open to influence. It should be made clear at the outset what service users may or may not be able to change.

Professionals are now interacting with service users as partners in strategic planning arenas as well as at frontline service delivery level. It appears that involving frontline staff in participation strategies and providing user-led awareness training could help improve relations at both strategic and service delivery level. The role of professional allies could be usefully explored.

Challenges to traditional professional modes of thinking and operating are emerging as a result of participation. Organisational cultures and structures need to respond and change in order to accommodate new partnerships and new ways of working with people who have often been oppressed and marginalised. The service user movement seems to be exposing the limitations of traditional, fragmented service categories for organising participation designed to promote strategic change. Participation provides a unique opportunity for organisations to develop through user-led critical enquiry using the social model of disability and ideas about control, oppression, rights, poverty and citizenship.

The extent of current knowledge

There is a general lack of research and evaluation on the impact and outcomes of service user participation. Little seems to be formally recorded at local, regional or national levels and the influence of user participation on transforming services has not been the subject of any major UK research studies to date.

There is some knowledge about participation techniques but little or no examination of the relationship between the process and the achievement of tangible user-led change. This is not to say that certain participation initiatives are not contributing to the improvement of services for the people who use them, rather that those changes are not being monitored.

Intrinsic benefits of participation

Where monitoring and evaluation is taking place, it is often related to participation processes rather than outcomes. Some agencies may only be focusing on the intermediate aspects of how individuals experience the process, rather than combining this evaluation with an assessment of impact and outcome. While intrinsic benefits are important, the true effectiveness of these processes to promote change and impact on improvement remains largely untested.

Feedback

Service users say they need to receive feedback as an integral part of the participation process, but this does not appear to be happening. Agencies should see monitoring of impact and meaningful feedback as a vital constituent of process, as it is related to engagement and commitment. When little or nothing is communicated back to participants, this can have a negative effect on their motivation, trust and confidence.

Participation and change at an individual level

Exercise of choice as an individual 'welfare consumer' remains restricted, particularly if you are from a black or ethnic minority group or are lesbian or gay. The ability to make choices can be limited by a lack of information about options and a lack of support for decision making. Professionally led assessment of eligibility for services can pose difficulties for exercising choice and control.

The implementation of direct payments by local authorities and the extent to which they are publicised is inconsistent. Good support systems, including access to advisors and peer support networks are needed. The limited choice and support has, in some cases, led to the establishment of user-controlled service providers and services by and for black and ethnic minority people.

Local authorities have formal complaints procedures intended to enable individuals to exercise some control over the quality of services. However, such procedures may not be functioning to the advantage of the service user or the agency. Complaints procedures can remain unknown, inaccessible or intimidating to service users.

Organisational commitment and responsiveness

Despite the overall lack of research or recorded knowledge illuminating the relationship between user participation and service change and improvement, the reviews show strong indications of why change may not be occurring. A lack of organisational responsiveness is an issue common to all the reviews. A fundamental political commitment to change should be driving participation initiatives.

Power relations

Power issues underlie the majority of identified difficulties with effective user-led change. User participation initiatives require continual awareness of the context of power relations in which they are being conducted. Exclusionary structures, institutional practices and professional attitudes can still affect the extent to which service users can influence change. It appears that power sharing can be difficult within established mainstream structures, formal consultation mechanisms and traditional ideologies.

The relative values placed on different types of expertise and language, and the professional assumptions about decision-making competence can make it difficult for users to be heard, or to make an impact on decisions. Managerial concern about achieving 'representativeness' (although not necessarily diversity in terms of race or sexuality) can also impede the progress of user-led change.

Partnership or consultancy?

User participation initiatives can be at risk of becoming externalised consultation processes to approve of professional service planning and policy proposals, rather than enabling service users to be integral partners for their formulation.

Embedded, continuous but varied participation approaches, which engage service users as partners in decision making, seem to have most potential for influencing change. Service users want to choose how they are represented. Agencies are recommended to re-examine their notion of service users who are thought to be 'hard to reach'. Some service users may lack structures of representation or the knowledge and support to empower them to participate.

Conflict and expectations

Dissatisfaction and even conflict may be an inevitable part of the user participation process. Service users and professionals can have conflicting priorities. Limited funds and service remits can restrain the degree to which service users may be able to influence changes in services. Organisations should be clear from the outset about what can and cannot be done as a result of participation, and the true extent of user influence in the given circumstances. Similarly, service users should be empowered to voice their limits and expectations.

Development of mutual understanding and trust takes time. Working to timetables determined without service users may result in the exclusion of some people or limit their effective participation. It is important for agencies to support and fund user groups to enable them to maintain their independence and critical function.

Diversity and marginalisation

Attention to the diversity of service users in terms of race, culture and sexuality is lacking both in mainstream services and participation initiatives. This relates to both diversity within user groups and the relative lack of knowledge about user participation for marginalised people. There are also difficulties for black and ethnic minority and lesbian and gay disabled people, who are also working on the margins of a predominantly white, culturally heterosexual user movement. The challenge to mainstream services is to creatively engage all marginalised peoples, the concerns of whom often extend beyond service provision, to creating positive social and political identities in the face of discrimination.

The full report will be available in Spring 2004 at www.scie.org.uk.

PART FOUR

Making a difference locally

Using CHI reviews to create a 'best practice' clinical audit department

Richard W Kuczyc

Background

The first Commission for Health Improvement (CHI) review was published in December 2000 and there have, to date, been 345 subsequent publications. The only overview on these reports was provided to us by CHI, under *Emerging Themes from 175 Clinical Governance Reviews*, published in November 2002. Although that paper generalised on the findings of CHI review, it did not specifically mention audit activity. In looking at the trusts that have been reviewed, I was able to identify 164 that were acute secondary care trusts providing district general hospital full spectrum activities. Of this cohort, only 11 trusts were identified as receiving a level 3 award for clinical audit activities.

It was felt that it was important to learn what constitutes a well-performing clinical audit department in view of CHI reviews. This was felt to be necessary because of the change of activity within the National Clinical Audit Programme. NICE had been responsible, until December 2002, for National Clinical Audit activity but has since turned that activity over to CHI. In July 2003, CHI launched its intentions for the new National Clinical Audit Programme and has since presented at conferences the general ideas and attitudes of how National Audit will be taken forward, under the auspices of CHI. Since the information given does not contain expectations of clinical audit departments, it was felt that a review of published data by CHI about audit activity would reveal key factors in creating a 'best practice' clinical audit department.

The study

The first part of the process was to review the clinical audit section of the 11 trusts that had been reviewed by CHI. This covered a time frame from February 2002 until May 2003. Therefore, the report format was somewhat different in several instances. The review was conducted by transcribing CHI comments into four categories. These were:

- positive comments
- negative comments
- notable comments
- action recommendations.

This produced a working study of 204 comments, of which 115 were positive, 33 were notable, 30 were negative and 26 were recommendations for action.

After review, the comments were grouped into general categories and two charts were produced (*see* Figures A and B). Figure A takes 'positive' and 'notable' comments and puts them into five categories. As you can observe, the two highest or most frequent comments were related to good communication and communication systems and ensuring that staff and health economy partners and users were involved in clinical audit activities.

Figure B takes the 'negative' comments, including the action referrals, and of these the two highest categories indicate few or no multiprofessional audits being carried out and poor access of audit information for trust members to review.

Due to the multiplicity and complexity of the statements, it was felt that the study needed to be carried a step further and an interview audit was designed.

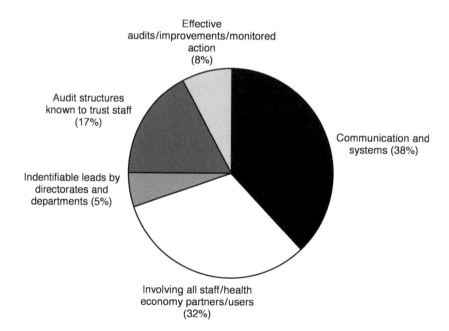

Figure A 'Positive' comments modified.

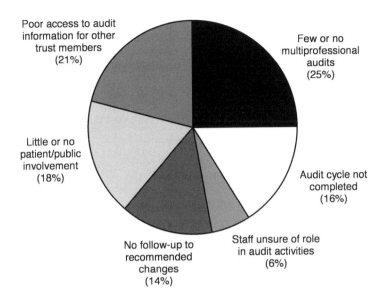

Figure B 'Negative' comments.

The audit

The clinical audit departments of the 11 trusts involved were called and a telephone interview questionnaire was designed containing 23 simple 'yes/no' questions. Seventeen of those questions were based on the finding from the CHI reports and six were based on personal experiences within the clinical audit departments. The questionnaire identified five areas of performance. These were:

1 structures in place, subdivided into clinical audit department structures
2 use and availability of information technology and management information
3 communications, primarily trustwide
4 audit involvement at a multiprofessional level and patient care user level
5 external issues, such as national surveys.

There were seven key issues on which there was total agreement across all of the interviewed respondents and these were:

1 they had a clinical audit strategy
2 they had methods, other than surveys, for patient involvement
3 there were formal methods set for presenting audits and audit outcomes
4 each department had a clinical audit database as well as additional databases, such as those involving guidelines and training activities

5   they had a system to distribute audit findings trustwide and they also had a system to distribute audit activity to the board and clinical governance committees
6   a full clinical audit training programme across the trust, was available to all staff
7   staff members of the clinical audit department had individually assigned directorate responsibilities.

Of lesser frequency, but of importance, was the fact that the clinical audit strategy in 75% of the cases was separate from the published clinical governance strategy and was a stand-alone document. Also of interest to note was that while all had formal methods of audit presentation a small percentage did not have methods of recording data about those presentations.

Two issues that received very mixed results were about protected time for audit for all staff. With the exception of one trust, which had no protected time, there was an even distribution between trusts that had protected time for everyone and those that had protected time for selected groups within the trust.

The series of questions focused on the clinical audit department's involvement with external activities that have, at times, been assigned to the department. The first question was about the administration of national surveys at an in-house level. Answers were divided into three very distinct categories – one-third involved themselves in the process of the national survey; one-third also involved themselves but shared that activity with other organisations within the trust; and one-third had taken on board the surveys. However, of those taking on board the surveys, each manager involved expressed a distinct self-interest in dealing with the national survey activity.

They were then asked about dissemination of NICE technological information. While all were in some way involved, the majority either had a single identified lead responsible within the department or shared the activity with other departments. A question was then asked regarding their involvement in NSFs and only two-thirds were involved to some degree, again either having an identified lead or a shared activity. Finally, they were asked about their involvement in essence of care and there was a very marked distinction, with 50% responding that they were involved and 50% responding very definitely that they were not.

Conclusions

Based on the findings, reports, investigations and interviews, it becomes apparent that there are five key issues instrumental in evolving a clinical audit department to 'best practice':

1   having good communication methods and systems in place, with easily identified strategies, methodology and sharing of outcomes from audits
2   ensuring the involvement of the staff, health economy partners and users.

This is especially brought forward in the use of multiprofessional and multi-departmental audits. Of special note was the ability to identify ways to bring healthcare economy partners into a sharing of lessons learned

3   having identifiable leads, by directorate and by department, which help in dissemination of audit planning, audit activity and monitoring of recommended changes made by the audits. This factor weighed very favourably in a positive activity

4   having good audit structures, across the trust, which are also well known and shared with all trust staff members

5   ensuring that audits are effective, that improvements can be identified and that actions against those improvements are monitored and sustained.

Similarly, areas of negativity that need to be corrected fall into six identifiable categories:

1   there is little or no multiprofessional auditing being done
2   the audit cycle is not being completed
3   staff are unsure of their roles in audit activities
4   there is no follow-up for recommended changes
5   there is little or no patient or public involvement
6   there is poor access to audit information for other trust members.

By using these findings and the original questions of the telephone interview, you can make a checklist of 'best practice'. This, in turn, could be used as a PDSA (plan, do, study, act) study of your current clinical audit department activity, resulting in notable areas for action and improvement.

Working together to manage risk

Sarah Williamson

Sheffield Teaching Hospitals was created on 1 April 2001 from two already large acute trusts – Central Sheffield University Hospitals and the Northern General Hospital. The new trust has two major campuses, one of which contains three hospitals. At the end of the first year post-merger a clinical governance manager and clinical risk manager were confirmed in post, reporting to the deputy medical director with responsibility for clinical governance.

Around the same time the appointment of a clinical governance pharmacist was made, and a strong working relationship has built up among these three people. The clinical governance manager and pharmacist are active members of the clinical risk infrastructure, which in itself provides strong links across risk and governance. Similar key relationships exist between clinical risk and infection control, professional development, radiology, medical physics and supplies, and are all reflected in the clinical risk committee structure.

The clinical governance manager, clinical risk manager and clinical governance pharmacist have acted as a task force to lead on several trustwide practice issues since the merger. The most significant have been: intrathecal chemotherapy, strong potassium and, most recently, anaesthetic medication labels.

In each case the approach has been similar, and the methods have become refined with practice. The core team of three has met together to review the external guidelines and assess in broad terms the current position of the trust. From this preliminary work more detailed questions have been formulated – about usage, storage, checking procedures, for instance, and the clinical governance pharmacist has fed these through her network of colleagues on all sites to ascertain our exact position and to identify areas where action needs to be taken. Actions identified through this process may be trustwide – introduction of a written procedure, perhaps – or local – solving a problem about storage.

This 'go and look' phase is a very important part of the process, and needs to involve very specific questions about practice. For instance, rather than asking: 'Is drug X stored securely?' you would ask: 'How is drug X stored?' Colleagues may not realise that long-standing procedures are now out of date and may in all sincerity tell you that practice is acceptable when it isn't. We have found this to be true of infection control and decontamination as well as medicines management.

Often this 'go and look' exercise will identify that there is a need to standardise practices across different sites and departments, and this is where the clinical governance and clinical risk managers can play their part, by meeting with colleagues representing different existing practices, and brokering acceptable solutions which satisfy both local and national requirements. This supports the clinical governance pharmacist by depersonalising the issues, and allowing a forum for equal debate which can be set in the wider context of governance as a whole, rather than as a contest between two points of view. Anyone who has lived through a merger, be it of trust or department, will know the tensions and understand that both parties can feel as though they are the subjects of a takeover. Using an overarching clinical governance approach can be helpful in moving the debate forward.

Another benefit of the 'go and look' approach is that you may well find pockets of activity no one knew about at the preliminary discussions, but which need to be brought into the action plan. It also allows the central team to gain a real understanding of the practical issues that have to be addressed in implementing new policy and guidelines, and obviously gives frontline staff the opportunity to contribute to planning and to shape implementation. In instituting new procedures for strong potassium, for instance, we were able to introduce new checking and recording procedures in areas where the first response was that the workload generated would be intolerable. The clinical governance pharmacist and clinical risk manager visited the areas, discussed the potential problems and advised on practical solutions. We also promised to monitor the situation and to take immediate alternative action if the foreseen difficulties actually transpired. A year on we have not received any complaints.

The pharmacy department itself was concerned about the potential workload associated with removal of strong potassium and the need to have special doses made up in pharmacy. In the event, thanks to raising awareness of the available ranges of pre-prepared potassium solutions, the pharmacy department has received only seven requests for made-up solutions since the policy was introduced. These requests are being reviewed for appropriateness, and in any case do not represent a major burden. It has been noticed that most were received out of hours, and fulfilled by junior pharmacists. In future such requests will be referred to a senior pharmacist for approval, and it is hoped this will reduce the requirement still further, as a senior pharmacist will be better placed to advise on the appropriate use of stock preparations.

This approach was also used in the introduction of new guidelines for intrathecal chemotherapy management, although those initiatives were confined to specific areas of the trust. Since then we have been able to respond quickly and effectively to further guidance as it appears, because the strong core team exists. For intrathecal chemotherapy and, more recently, for the introduction of national anaesthetic drug labels, the core team has been augmented by appropriate specialist staff. In the case of anaesthetic drug labelling, it has happened in some trusts that anaesthetic departments have chosen to implement the recommendations without wider discussion within their own trust – we were able to pick up this issue and ensure that it was managed cohesively across the whole trust.

The advantage of this approach, and of the high profile of the clinical governance pharmacist within clinical risk activity, is that we are more likely to be made aware of practice changes and potential problems of all kinds, and are able to put an effective rapid response mechanism in place.

A strategic approach to clinical governance

Charlette Middlemiss

Introduction

In this presentation I will describe how the development of a strategic approach to clinical governance is influencing changes and improvements to clinical services. A corporate initiative and two case studies will be presented to demonstrate the benefits that resulted from the implementation of clinical governance.

Revising the previous clinical governance strategy provided an opportunity to place greater emphasis on the approaches needed to support the implementation of clinical governance. The original strategy focused on setting out work to support the development of systems and processes for managing clinical governance. With this work successfully completed, the need to review the strategy in order to introduce renewed impetus became clear as discussions, particularly with frontline staff, began to focus more on the delivery aspects of clinical governance.

Background

The creation of two new corporate posts designed specifically to support the implementation process is a key feature of the strategy. Working with clinical teams on various initiatives, these posts are helping to change what clinical teams do, and the way they work. Mercer describes the implementation of clinical governance as requiring a long-term, bottom-up, 'softly softly' approach, as opposed to quick fixes.[1] The philosophy underpinning the work of the patient experience facilitator and the clinical governance co-ordinator places emphasis on involving people and engaging them in reviewing clinical practices and achieving clinical improvement and effective clinical governance. The focus is to nurture a sense of ownership, trust and voluntary engagement of staff at all levels by applying facilitative, developmental and supportive approaches to change.[2-6]

Bro Morgannwg NHS Trust is one of the largest trusts in Wales, providing integrated healthcare services to a population of around 300 000. The quality agenda has always been a high priority. This has provided a good foundation for developing a strategic approach to both the development and implementation of clinical governance.

The purpose of the new strategy is to offer direction and leadership by using clinical governance as a driver to modernise clinical services and drive up quality of care across the organisation. The overarching principles are:

- to ensure that clinical governance arrangements underpin all clinical activities and are taken forward cohesively and consistently across all services
- to identify and agree priorities for the clinical governance development plan
- to highlight challenges and constraints that may impact on the clinical governance agenda and identify solutions.

Putting patients at the centre and valuing the contributions of frontline staff are key to the success of these principles. Effective leadership by clinicians responsible for improving the quality of care to patients, coupled with commitment and support from managers, is required if clinical governance is to succeed.[7] A devolved management structure and an organisational culture, which encourages frontline staff to develop creative solutions to problems, provided a good foundation for supporting the following initiatives to be taken forward.

Corporate initiative

Patients, users and carers are becoming increasingly involved in shaping and influencing the delivery of care. Working with patients and capturing their experiences is the cornerstone of modernising healthcare. Patient participation and involvement is therefore crucial to clinical governance.

The appointment of a trust patient experience facilitator to support the strategic and operational developments of the patient and public involvement agenda has had a significant impact on improving the experience of patients within the trust. The patient experience facilitator works directly with clinical teams to develop meaningful and proactive approaches to patient and public involvement. The development of a trust-wide suggestion scheme and the ward visit programme have been two strands of work in particular which, when coupled to a comprehensive consumer care programme, have had a positive impact on the delivery of services across the trust.

Trust suggestion scheme

The clinical encounter between a patient and a healthcare professional is a core activity in delivering care. Increasingly, attention is being paid to patients' views on care, and to developing a more patient-centred approach. The developing and implementation of a suggestion scheme to elicit service user comments has been influential in making a difference for patients.

The focus of the scheme was initially to hear the voices of those patients – members of the public who would not traditionally comment on their care for a number of reasons. The scheme was developed from the outset with patient involvement both in terms of the structure of the scheme and the design of leaflets and posters – this was to maximise the impact and ensure a good response rate.

After two years of development, the trust received 350 suggestions last year and 298 in the first six months of this year. Each leaflet where contact details are provided is responded to. Feedback is given where appropriate.

Now that the volumes have developed, the scheme is highlighting trends and deficiencies that can be acted upon. In addition it has been pleasing to receive a significant number of positive comments that have helped to maintain staff morale.

An example where the scheme has made a difference is within the accident and emergency department. This is a very busy department dealing with over 93 000 admissions per year. A number of suggestions received indicated that patients were expressing concerns regarding poor communication by staff and lack of information.

Working with the clinical team, the patient experience facilitator delivered targeted training sessions designed to improve the interface between staff, patients and the public. When this was linked to work relating to access to services and patient flow through the department, the results improved significantly. Positive comments continue to be received about the care environment and the attitude of staff.

Ward visit programme

The aim of the ward visit programme is to look at the environment of care through the eyes of a patient. The approach focuses on an objective, observational assessment of the clinical area.

The visit programme forms the third and final part of an integrated programme to improve the patient experience across the trust. The stages involve:

- stage 1: a 30-minute induction session for all new staff joining the trust to introduce the importance of patient experience and to emphasise the role each member of staff has in making a difference
- stage 2: a series of interactive customer care sessions to develop the themes introduced in stage 1. These workshops are targeted at contact staff, managers and supervisors within clinical directorates
- stage 3: the ward visit programme to evaluate the effect of training and to review issues such as:

- standards of hygiene
- information available to patients
- standards of maintenance
- access to medical equipment
- interactions between professionals and the patient.

The methodology used follows the proforma adapted from the hospital patient environment action team visits undertaken by the community health councils (CHCs) in Wales similar to the patient environment action team (PEAT) project in England. However, the methodology is supplemented with observations similar to those used by the RCN Clinical Leadership Programme and comments received from patients. A report and action plan is produced following each visit, which is then used to support change and improvement.

Following a recent stage 2 workshop, staff from an assessment ward were enthusiastic about making changes and improvements to the care environment. The patient experience facilitator subsequently visited the unit and, through working with the clinical team, highlighted a number of issues including:

- organisation of staff on the unit to ensure a balance of smooth running and patient interface
- aspects of maintenance of the environment of care that were not acceptable
- issues of poor signage and patient information
- storage facilities.

An action plan was developed and submitted, and within a short period of time all issues were addressed, leading to an improved patient environment and working environment for staff. In addition the initiative reinforced to clinical staff and managers in particular a number of fundamental issues, including the importance of property maintenance, which can have a direct impact on patient care.

Clinical governance case summaries

From a clinical governance perspective, empowering staff to be creative and learn will in turn help them to develop innovative ideas for new ways of working. The following two case summaries will demonstrate how patients and staff have benefited from the introduction of new ways of working.

Case summary 1: an initiative to extend the roles and responsibilities of physiotherapists

Orthopaedic consultants refer more patients to physiotherapy than any other specialist. A physiotherapist can work as a first-line filter system for certain patients who may not require surgical intervention. In addition a physiotherapist has greater familiarity with instructing patients about self-help of chronic conditions. Against this background, and the local need to streamline and improve access to treatment, the clinical team set about changing the traditional model of care provided. Two physiotherapists underwent training and development to enable them to undertake certain elements of care which fell outside the conventional scope of physiotherapy practice, for example requesting investigations and using the results to make a clinical diagnosis and determine appropriate clinical management. Outcome benefits from this initiative include the following:

- reduced outpatient waiting times for patients
- reduced orthopaedic outpatient waiting list
- facilitated effective management
- reduction of the number of referrals
- improved communication between primary and secondary care
- patients are empowered to help themselves in the management of chronic musculoskeletal conditions
- released time for orthopaedic medical staff to focus on surgical cases.

In addition the results from a patient satisfaction survey highlighted that 99% of patients felt that they were participating fully in determining the future management of their condition.

The experience gained from the implementation of this initiative in orthopaedics has been shared with staff providing care to rheumatology patients, to support the introduction of a new model of service provision that it is anticipated will achieve similar outcome benefits.

Case summary 2: the introduction of laughter therapy

One of the day hospitals in the trust has developed a unique approach for supporting mental health patients through the establishment of a laughter therapy workshop. The occupational therapist and nurse who run the workshop advocate that laughter is an antidote to anxiety and stress.

They emphasise the importance of integrating laughter into patient contacts. A six-week course comprising weekly two-hour sessions is accessed directly by patients. The aim of the course is to encourage and teach people to get laughter into their lives. Although this is a new and different approach, the clinical governance benefits found from this unique initiative are apparent:

- it offers patients an alternative choice of treatment
- it empowers service users to self-refer

- the workshop saves time, staff numbers and shortens patients' length of stay, as it combines a number of therapy courses into one
- it treats multiple patients at once through group work
- patients continue their own treatment independently and with other members of the group, when not attending the group
- the patients are more motivated and compliant with other treatments
- the therapy has a by-product effect on carers and fellow patients
- the clinical team enjoy providing the workshop, which is improving team working.

The clinical team responsible for this initiative maintains that laughter has many emotional and physical benefits and is the body's natural resource for combating mental and physical ill health. Several other clinical specialities have expressed an interest in this work. There are plans to extend its application to benefit other groups of patients in the future, e.g. stroke and palliative care patients.

Conclusion

Walshe and colleagues state that so far clinical governance has made little real difference in NHS trusts and, at best, there is only a growing awareness of clinical governance ideas among clinicians. They further argue that attention should focus at a service level in order to equip clinicians with the skill and support they need, providing structures and processes at directorate, speciality and departmental level to take clinical governance forward.[8] The NHS Executive (1998) reported that clinical governance 'could become a bureaucratic extravaganza, without much effect on the quality of patient care'.[9] These initiatives demonstrate how clinical governance can become a reality when it changes the way that clinicians or professions see their own involvement in quality improvement. These creative approaches have enabled frontline staff to make real changes to the way that their services are delivered, which is producing real improvements in the quality of care for patients.

Applying a strategic approach to the implementation of clinical governance is essential to ensure sustainable quality improvement. Clinical governance is a long-term initiative, which needs to be supported at all levels. The contribution from staff directly and indirectly involved in the delivery of care has a significant impact on the patient's experience. It is important therefore that all staff feel a sense of ownership and engagement in the planning and discussions relating to service delivery, development and improvement.

These examples of clinical governance initiatives undertaken within the trust demonstrate how simple changes can make a real difference to the experiences of patients.

References

1   Mercer SW and Reynolds WJ (2002) Empathy and quality of care. *British Journal of General Practice* **10**: QS, S9.

2   Sweeney G, Stead J, Sweeney K and Greco M (2001) Exploring the implementation and development of clinical governance in primary care within the South West region: views from PCG clinical governance leads. wisdomnet.co.uk/cgmenu.html, accessed February 2001.

3   Sweeney GM, Sweeney KG, Greco MJ and Stead JW (2002) Softly, softly, the way forward? A qualitative study of the first year of implementing clinical governance in primary care. *Primary Health Research and Development* **3**: 53–64.

4   Campbell SM, Roland MO and Wilkin D (2001) Improving the quality of care through clinical governance. *British Medical Journal* **322**: 1580–2.

5   Campbell SM, Sheaff R, Sibbald B *et al.* (2002) Implementing clinical governance in English primary care groups/trusts: reconciling quality improvement and quality assurance. *Quality in Health Care* **11**: 9–14.

6   Sweeney G, Sweeney K, Greco M and Stead J (2001) Moving clinical governance forward: capturing the experiences of primary care group leads. *Clinical Governance Bulletin* **2 (1)**: 6–7.

7   Campbell S, Roland M and Wilkin D (2001) Improving the quality of care through clinical governance. *British Medical Journal* **322**: 1580–2.

8   Walshe K, Freeman T, Latham L, Wallace L and Spurgeon P (2000) *Clinical Governance: from policy to practice.* University of Birmingham: Birmingham. www.bham.ac.uk/lsmc

9   Berwick DM (1996) A primer on leading the improvements of systems. *British Medical Journal* **312**: 619–22.

Reducing health inequalities

Paul Seviour

In his foreword to the Department of Health publication, *Tacking Health Inequalities: a programme for action*, the Prime Minister, Tony Blair, states:

> Our society remains scarred by inequalities. Whole communities remain cut off from the greater wealth and opportunities that others take for granted. This, in turn, fuels avoidable health inequalities.[1]

South Ward, Weston-super-Mare, is one such community. When taking into account six areas of deprivation (income, employment, health and disability, education skills and training, housing, geographical access to services), South Ward ranks in the bottom 6% of all wards in England and is more than 7500 places below another ward in the same PCT area.

After a health needs assessment in 1998 the local CHC concluded that the area needed a full-time dedicated general practice, services specific to the needs of young people, health promotion activities related to chronic disease and action on lifestyle issues such as drugs and alcohol.

The Weston Personal Medical Services (PMS) Pilot opened its doors to patients for the first time in April 2000. The primary healthcare team (PHCT) was recruited by panels of both professionals and local residents. The lay people were facilitated in this by representatives of the CHC. The partnership between professionals and local residents has continued since, with the establishment of a healthy living project. Currently in construction is a £2.5 million Healthy Living Centre which has been funded through the New Opportunities Fund, together with the five partners, comprising North Somerset Council, North Somerset PCT, Sure Start, Anglican/Methodist church and the Bournville Community Association. Local residents are in the majority with respect to management of the centre.

In its first three years the PMS Pilot has grown and now serves the needs of 2500 patients. As a consequence of the characteristics of the local population and the nature of the social housing, the population is turning over at nearly 50% per year. This leads one to ask who are the 'local' population and how do we engage them in planning the services? The work the PHCT did in the PMS Pilot in the first two years was rewarded by their coming first in a national competition for teams working to reduce health inequalities.

In *Tackling Health Inequalities* the government identifies four themes in its programme for action:

- supporting families, mothers and children
- engaging communities and individuals
- preventing illness and providing treatment
- addressing the underlying determinants of health.[1]

The PHCT has done much work in the first three of these themes. Access to health services has been improved for the local community and particularly for young families. The age profile of the practice population is very different from those of neighbouring practices, with a third of the patients being under 16 years old. Young families are supported by health visitors and now also by Sure Start. Fifteen children have been on the child protection register in the year ending March 2003, with a further 33 classed as 'in need'. The principles of advanced access are applied to the practice and the nursing team is running minor illness clinics on a daily basis.

Many people have engaged with health services on a regular basis for the first time. This has particularly been the case for those misusing drugs and alcohol. Of the practice population, 5% are known to be past or present heroin users. Many of these have young families. The practice has been supported in its delivery of services to drug and alcohol misusers by the local specialist team. A shared care scheme operates very successfully and safely in Weston-Super-Mare. The practice is also providing services to those who are registered locally as 'violent patients'. A nurse member of the PHCT is engaging and supporting young people in the local community by means of a weekly drop-in clinic based at the practice premises and also by contacts made in the local schools.

Like any other general practice, much of the day-to-day work of the PHCT is in preventing illness and providing treatment. Members of the nursing team are trained to support people to stop smoking. In the year ending March 2003, 57 people had set a quit date and 23 had still quit by four weeks. There is still much to be done here with 62% of active asthmatics, 29% of diabetics and 30% of patients with coronary heart disease still smoking. Nurse-led clinics have been established for coronary heart disease, asthma and diabetes. The practice has a policy of selective screening for diabetes and has a current prevalence of 3.3% (4.7% of the adult population). Obesity is a major problem, with 54% of diabetics having a body mass index greater than 30.

How can the PHCT address the underlying determinants of health and is this its role? The government admits that the actions likely to have the greatest impact on health inequalities include:

- improved social housing and reduced fuel poverty
- improved educational attainment
- reduced unemployment and improved income among the poorest.[1]

In their analysis, Mitchell, Dorling and Shaw calculated the number of lives that could be saved by successful implementation of three government policies, i.e. mild redistribution of wealth, achievement of full employment and eradication of child poverty.[2] In the whole of Britain, 10% of all deaths in the under-65s could be prevented by these policies. In areas with above average mortality, 56% of all deaths in the under-65s could be prevented in this way.

In *Tackling Health Inequalities* the government details its strategy for addressing these underlying determinants of health.[1]

The Healthy Living Project and the PHCT working within it tackles inequalities at an individual, group or community level. It will recognise local priorities and seek to deliver services in an appropriate, innovative and equitable way.

References

1 Department of Health (2003) *Tacking Health Inequalities: a programme for action*. Department of Health: London.

2 Mitchell R, Dorling D and Shaw M (2000) *Inequalities in Life and Death: what if Britain were more equal?* The Policy Press: Bristol.

Making clinical governance work at the front line

Sean O'Kelly

Clinical governance is traditionally characterised as a framework by which NHS organisations are accountable for continuously improving the quality of their services and safeguarding high standards of care by creating an environment in which excellence will flourish. For frontline clinicians however, clinical governance needs to grow from a definition into something tangible that helps them achieve this on a day-to-day basis in their clinical practice. The National Clinical Governance Development Programme was initiated with this objective in mind. This programme, delivered by the National Clinical Governance Support Team, teaches a methodology for change that is grounded in the essential themes of clinical governance, yet remains a practical and successful way of ensuring that clinical governance happens at the front line of medical care. This short paper will introduce some of the essentials of this methodology and explain why it is an appropriate focus for those who work at the front line.

RAID methodology

RAID (review, agree, implement, demonstrate) has developed from the key clinical governance themes of ownership, leadership, teamwork and communication. It is a practical and engaging way of bringing about the changes needed to improve clinical services and is accomplished by frontline clinical staff working together. RAID programmes have been implemented widely throughout the health service and have led to many examples of successfully improved clinical services.

Each step on the RAID path is not a discrete entity but merges into the next one in what amounts to a continuous improvement process. Briefly, each part of the RAID process can be summarised as follows:

- *Review*: the review is a comprehensive information-gathering process which includes obtaining the views both of staff involved with the service and the users of the service. Staff are thereby given ownership of the change process at an early stage and are consequently much more likely to be helpful and active when it comes to the implementation and maintenance of specific service changes. Other useful information about the subject or service in question can also be obtained from audit and by seeking out relevant existing documentation.

- *Agree*: the agreement phase begins towards the end of the review, when those leading the process draw out a consensus as to what needs to be changed in order to build a higher quality service. Depending on the nature and scope of the project, a number of specific recommendations for change may be agreed upon at this stage. Agreement is most likely when projects chosen have a degree of overlap with the overall objectives of the organisation or service under review.
- *Implement*: during the implementation phase the recommendations for change are put into practice by teams each dealing with a specific project. Project management allows specific objectives to be planned on a specific timescale with change then happening step by step, project by project. Effective communication and teamwork are the keys to successful project management.
- *Demonstrate*: this phase encourages the measurement and communication of successful changes to clinical services. It also allows for a period of reflective learning when performance can be assessed and lessons learned for further change initiatives.

Change within the health service can be a difficult process and there are many reasons why this has been so. However, in order for the quality of clinical care to improve, changes must be contemplated and then effected. Fortunately our understanding of how complex systems such as the health service behave has improved and we are now in a better position to influence change than before. Top-down change in the health service has often been regarded with a degree of concern by those at the bottom of the service hierarchy and in the front line of clinical care. There are many reasons why change initiated in this way may become dissipated and ineffective as it moves down through the system, or may be inherently irrelevant to the needs of frontline workers and patients from the outset. RAID gives us a tool that helps promote smaller but multiple bottom-up change initiatives, designed, implemented and sustained by those who know the service and the service users best. When RAID works well, a group of frontline workers develop a collective knowledge of the service they provide beyond that held by any individual. This knowledge is used to generate specific ideas about areas of the service that become the focus of the change process. RAID produces an enthusiasm and commitment among frontline workers and delivers a mandate for change that is difficult to resist. RAID can help liberate frontline staff who feel the need to be involved with service improvement but who might otherwise find difficulty organising and expressing this desire. Once the service has been reshaped so that quality is enhanced, the RAID process helps ensure continued support for the changed service and a continued emphasis on further service development.

Making clinical governance work at the front line is a significant challenge to all those involved in healthcare, but one that must be met if the quality of care enjoyed by patients is to be improved. Without a process that allows frontline clinical workers to engage with, arrange and carry through change, this challenge would be daunting. Clinical governance belongs at the front line of healthcare and the RAID process is perhaps the best way of ensuring that this is where it is found.

Further reading

- Halligan A and Donaldson L (2001) Implementing clinical governance: turning vision into reality. *British Medical Journal* **322**: 1413–17.
- National Audit Office (2003) *Achieving Improvements through Clinical Governance.* Report by the Comptroller and Auditor General. HC 1055 Session 2002–2003: 17 September 2003. National Audit Office: London.
- Plsek P and Greenhalgh T (2001) The challenge of complexity in health care. *British Medical Journal* **323**: 625–8.

National Clinical Audit 2002–2004

Jenifer Smith

Sir Ian Kennedy's report on the deaths occurring among some children under-going heart surgery at the Bristol Royal Infirmary elicited a response from the Secretary of State for Health to establish an Office for Information on Healthcare Performance.[1] This became a reality during 2002, with the CHI being given responsibility for, among other things:

- guiding and funding a programme of national clinical audit
- publishing standards for national clinical audit and endorsing projects against these.

In an ideal world, one would determine a strategy for a programme of national clinical audit, reflecting the principles one would wish to employ in 'guiding' such a programme, then commission work programmes according to this. As in other aspects of the health service though, this was not a clean start and there was some work in progress to be secured before further progress could be made on the future picture. Initial activity focused on maintaining activity within those projects either being, or expecting to be, funded by NICE during 2002. Progress was rapidly made in establishing agreements with the relevant professional bodies to take forward national clinical audit projects covering:

- the administration of thrombolytic treatment to those suffering a myocardial infarction
- the management of venous ulcers in community settings
- the management of violence within mental healthcare settings
- stroke care.

Details of these and other national clinical audit projects funded by CHI can be found on the clinical audit and surveys section of the website.[2]

Alongside this, work began on future arrangements for national clinical audits in diabetes, evidence-based prescribing in the elderly and parenteral nutrition. In the case of the latter, it was decided that the National Patient Safety Agency could more appropriately lead the necessary work programme.

After a period of discussion with stakeholders it was decided to tender for a national clinical audit to support appropriate prescribing of aspirin, benzodiazepines, biphosphonates, oral hypoglycaemics and bronchodilators in the elderly. The lessons learnt from the project funded to develop quality indicators for diabetes services (QUIDS) were used to form the basis of a national clinical audit within the programme to support the implementation of the NSFs (see below).

Perhaps in part because there had been no clear focus for policy development of this activity within the Department of Health (DoH), national clinical audit projects were being commissioned through a variety of routes apart from NICE, with sponsors both within the DoH and elsewhere. A very large National Clinical Audit Support Programme (NCASP) was initiated, intended to support, among other things, monitoring the implementation of NSFs for cancer, coronary heart disease and diabetes. This was being commissioned from the NHS Information Authority. Responsibility for commissioning this transferred to the CHI in April 2003.

It is hoped that priorities for funding future projects will be assessed within a matrix incorporating:

- clinical priorities as determined by the DoH
- the relationship between the volume of activity undertaken and the risk of harm to patients through inappropriate care
- practitioners primarily involved
- requirements of the healthcare regulator (CHI/CHAI).

Opportunities for strengthening national clinical audit

Securing the existing work programmes confirmed the need for a common framework of standards within which national clinical audit could develop, whatever the source of funding. In determining what those standards should cover, the CHI was mindful that clinical audit has been criticised in the past for not delivering sufficient improvements in patient care to justify the substantial time, effort and money devoted to it.[3] It would be important to draw on:

- evidence within the literature for characteristics of clinical audit projects which had successfully improved patient care
- evidence documented as part of CHI's extensive programme of clinical governance reviews of how effectively healthcare organisations were embedding clinical audit within their clinical governance arrangements
- deficiencies of clinical audit identified in *Learning from Bristol.*[1]

The publication *Principles for Best Practice in Clinical Audit* is a good source for the evidence base supporting characteristics of a successful clinical audit.[4] This makes it clear that one must pay attention to both the technical aspects of an audit project itself and the characteristics of the environment within which this is to be carried out. In the past this would have been difficult to achieve within the national clinical audit programme, but linking with the clinical governance reviews carried out by CHI and the programme of inspections to be undertaken by the new health regulator, CHAI, offer an exciting opportunity to improve the effectiveness of the national clinical audit programme. Clinical audits will be assessed under a scheme for endorsing national clinical audits against specified standards covering:

- relevance of topics to clinical priorities and clinical practice
- robust methodology, including applicability to quality improvement, data and statistical issues, database management, justification for measures of risk adjustment
- information governance
- clinical, managerial and public/patient ownership
- value for money
- project management and delivery.

The following recurrent themes emerge in statements made by review teams assessing the competence of organisational arrangements for clinical audit:

- lack of patient and service user involvement
- disparity between the clinical audit programme and the clinical governance priorities
- insufficient multidisciplinary engagement
- patchy training for staff
- incomplete implementation of action plans to address audit findings and disseminate good practice.

Future work

To help those wanting to ensure that future clinical audit projects comply with standards required to maximise the ability to improve patient care, a series of guidance papers will be produced and placed on the CHI website.[2] The first of these to be produced, and already available, cover project planning and statistical issues to be addressed when calculating risk adjusted outcome indicators. These are intended to be widely applicable and to be used in the same manner as one might use a checklist to remind oneself of what should be included. The more detailed assessment of how well the standards have been adhered to will be done through a system of 'peer review', provided we can satisfactorily resolve the issues of quality control within the peer reviewers and potential conflicts of interest which may arise when selecting peer reviewers from a comparatively small group involved in designing national clinical audit projects.

The national clinical audit programme will be an integral part of CHAI in April 2004. The vision for this organisation suggests that work already underway to strengthen the involvement of patients at all stages of this programme, linking with the programme of patient surveys to include the dimension of patient experience, and commissioning a programme to incorporate patient-assessed outcome, will ensure national clinical audit has a bright future within the regulation of healthcare.

References

1   HMSO (2001) *The Report of the Public Inquiry into Children's Heart Surgery at the Bristol Royal Infirmary 1984–1995. Learning from Bristol.* The Stationery Office: London.

2   www.chi.nhs.uk

3   HMSO (1995) *Clinical Audit in England.* The Stationery Office: London.

4   NICE (2002) *Principles for Best Practice in Clinical Audit.* Radcliffe Medical Press: Oxford.

Using patient and public involvement to improve the quality agenda at a local level

Damian Jenkinson

Introduction

Considering service users' views when planning and improving any clinical service is an essential part of modern healthcare. As experts on their illness, patients can do much to improve the quality of healthcare services and thus their involvement in strategies to change care provision is essential.

Service user participation is especially key to the development and provision of high-quality stroke care. People who suffer stroke, and their carers, are a particularly vulnerable group: typically older people, often with pre-existing physical impairments and disability. Their needs are complex, requiring input from multiple healthcare professions within the NHS. Moreover, stroke will leave as many as 60% of all sufferers with some degree of impairment of communication, making participation and involvement all the more challenging.[1]

The National Clinical Governance Support Programme for stroke employs service user participation as one of the core methods to improve the quality agenda at a local level, and provides a range of techniques to ensure users can participate as equal partners.

Stroke services: the need for change

Evidence from the Royal College of Physicians' National Sentinel Audit of Stroke suggests that progress and development of stroke services across the UK is unacceptably slow, with marked variation across the UK in terms of the organisation and process of care.[2] In 1999, just 25% of stroke patients spent most of their time on a stroke unit and by 2002 this had risen to only 27%.

The National Clinical Guidelines for Stroke emphasise the involvement of users, carers and families at two distinct levels.[3] First, stroke sufferers and their carers need to be involved in taking decisions regarding their own care. Second, the perceptions of service users are an important way of evaluating service delivery, and hence plans for service development should include the opinions of patients and carers.

The National Clinical Governance Support Programme for Stroke

The National Clinical Governance Support Programme for Stroke was created through collaborative working between the Stroke Association, the Royal College of Physicians and the NHS Clinical Governance Support Team.[4] The programme consists of five learning days over nine months, with agreed key actions during the intervals. Multi-agency teams from across health communities perform a review of their stroke services using the review, agree, implement and demonstrate (RAID) model. During the review phase, teams seek information regarding their existing services from current and past service users and carers, plus key clinical stakeholders, in addition to information from national and local audit and through process mapping.

Principles of user involvement in stroke

The core principles of user involvement are shown in Box A and are essentially the same in stroke as for other clinical areas. The particular challenges for involving users in stroke relate to the pre-existing vulnerability of this user group and the high incidence of communication disability after stroke.

Box A   Core principles of user involvement

- Involve at earliest opportunity
- Continuous collaboration
- Active participation as equal partners
- Work to define issues and identify solutions
- Develop capacity to participate

There is no one right way to involve patients, carers and service users. Methods should be matched to the task to hand. A range of tools and techniques is available (*see* Box B). The different levels of participation will capture the patients' experience differently and there may also be a number of approaches operating at the same time in any organisation.

Box B   Techniques to involve service users

- Patient advice and liaison services (PALS)
- Patient satisfaction monitoring
- Patient interviews
- Patient focus groups
- Patients' council
- Patient diaries
- Patient tracking

Experiences from the programme

One-hundred and fifty delegates from 33 trusts have completed the first three waves of the programme and a further nine are presently participating in the fourth. Evidence of improved user involvement was universally reported.

Common themes reported from many sites included the dispelling of staff anxieties that their work would be criticised when users were consulted, the realisation by staff that user demands would frequently differ from those predicted by staff and that the demands could often be met in a simple and quick manner. Of particular note was the involvement of patients with significant language impairment: teams reported that dysphasia did not restrict contributions, as long as there was an appropriate pace of explanation and adequate time for expression was given.

At Worcestershire Acute Hospitals NHS Trust the delegates undertook a patient satisfaction survey employing a new questionnaire agreed by their stroke team. Users were involved in the creation of the questionnaire and helped in its administration. Twenty inpatients (one with dysphasia) were interviewed over three months and their responses were used to create recommendations which are being incorporated into service delivery by the team: examples include counsellors to address emotional changes after stroke, seven-day therapy using multiskilled generic assistants and users being more involved in their care plans.

The team at the Royal Cornwall Hospitals NHS Trust were concerned that when they had attempted to involve users in a hospital setting on previous occasions, the users had been outnumbered by professionals and hence had been reluctant to contribute. The delegates addressed this by creating alternate-monthly patient and carer meetings across three PCTs and held in the community. Users were invited to attend by the local branch of the Stroke Association, the latter also facilitating discussions about existing stroke services and views on future developments.

The same delegates set up the Truro Dysphasic Group, which now holds a long-term exercise class to which users can refer themselves, and from which they can take away a personalised video of recommended post-stroke therapy. Lastly, this team created a telephone helpline for stroke, in partnership with the British Red Cross: the latter trained volunteers, filtered calls and managed the service.

At Tower Hamlets Healthcare NHS Trust, the team helped create a younger local users group, and in their rehabilitation unit, a key worker facilitates user involvement during goal setting.

At Winchester and Eastleigh NHS Trust, 150 questionnaires were circulated to service users by post, hand-to-hand and by email. Following comments received, written information for users has been revised and a patient and carer diary has been created for daily communication with staff on their unit. A discharge pack has been created, which includes a sheet given to each patient providing names and contact numbers for each health and social services agency that will be involved with their care after discharge.

Conclusions

User participation is crucial to the provision of high-quality stroke care, enhancing not only the care provided to individuals but helping fashion services that patients want and deserve. The National Clinical Governance Support Programme for Stroke provides training in a range of techniques to guarantee local user involvement. Despite the significant communication problems encountered by many patients after stroke, experiences from the programme demonstrate that they are surmountable and that effective communication with real listening to users can be accomplished.

References

1   Walker AE, Robins M and Weinfeld MD (1981) The National Survey of Stroke. *Stroke* **12** (2): 13–44.

2   Royal College of Physicians (Intercollegiate Stroke Working Party) (2001/2002) *National Sentinel Audit for Stroke*. Royal College of Physicians: London.

3   Royal College of Physicians (2003) *National Clinical Guidelines for Stroke*. Royal College of Physicians: London.

4   www.cgsupport.org/Programmes/Supporting_Stroke_Services

Local mental health commissioning: issues and practice

Ian Allured and John Hall

Commissioning practice with respect to mental health services has changed over the past few years, and patterns of joint commissioning now vary widely for a number of reasons, including:

- the publication of the NSF for Adult Mental Health in 1999 (and the associated policy implementation guidance)
- the change from the previous health authority-led processes to the new PCT-led processes, following *Shifting the Balance of Power*[1]
- the creation of large dedicated mental health NHS trusts from the previous mixed pattern of dedicated mental health, community and general hospital trusts
- the emergence of closer working between health and social care, leading to the new Section 31 arrangements.

These complex patterns of partnership, together with historical variations in provision, mean that there can be substantial differences in the services provided to different communities and groups within the same provider trust and strategic health authority areas, particularly to vulnerable subgroups. The challenge to PCTs and their local partners is to fulfil their commissioning role more effectively and so improve service quality and reduce inequity, although they may not possess the capacity and expertise in knowledge of population need and commissioning practice.

The Health and Social Care Advisory Service (HASCAS) has been awarded Section 64 funding from the DoH for a project to work with PCTs on their commissioning arrangements for adult mental health services. Expressions of interest were sought from PCTs, and from 29 initial expressions of interest, a carefully selected country-wide sample of nine PCTs has been selected, to include some with high proportions of black and ethnic minority residents, and with prisons. We have set up an expert steering group to guide the project, and we are now halfway through reviewing the commissioning procedures of this cohort.

The review process is structured around two sets of service development frameworks, one to review the commissioning arrangements themselves, and one to review compliance with the NSF. These frameworks are based on relevant evidence, policy and good practice, and each has around 20 main standard statements, with from five to ten criteria for each statement.

They have been developed from pre-existing HASCAS standards to conform to best practice in service standards design. The reviews are conducted over two or three days by a review team with a minimum of five members, which always includes a service user or carer, a commissioner and a HASCAS service development advisor, and others drawn from, for example, a general adult psychiatrist, a social services mental health managers, or a GP.

Each PCT receives an individual report on the review visit, which provides a benchmark of where they were considered to be against the standards, and which provides some recommendations on how the commissioning process can be improved. When all nine individual reports have been produced, a composite report will be published for the DoH which will highlight any lessons with a national significance, and suggest ways in which commissioning might be improved. The service development frameworks will themselves be amended in the light of this field testing.

HASCAS will be incorporating questionnaire-obtained views of service users and carers from each PCT by early in 2004. Each of the nine PCTs will be revisited to see whether they have altered their commissioning arrangements as a result of the recommendations in their individual report following the 2003 review. HASCAS will seek to start work with a second cohort of PCTs during 2004, and will be holding workshops to help PCTs with their commissioning.

From the reviews so far completed, and from other related work HASCAS is carrying out, a number of provisional findings are already apparent:

- the levels of knowledge and experience of mental health commissioners, and their ability to contribute throughout the overall commissioning cycle, vary widely. There is real need for training and support for new commissioners, and the regional development centres are addressing this need
- there are good-quality service-relevant research articles on commissioning appearing in a number of publications, such as the *Journal of Mental Health* and *Primary Care Mental Health*. These are not accessible to commissioners, and hence do not inform practice
- for many PCTs the move from health authorities, with a reduction in the capacity of the public health function, has meant reduced access to good-quality information about the mental health needs of their population
- service development frameworks are best seen as one flexible component in a process of practice improvement, rather than as a prescribed rigid inspectorial tool
- for low-volume, high-cost (and often high-risk) services, such as for those

with eating disorders or complex severe mental illness, the needs of users may be best met by county- or SHA-wide collaboration between PCTs

- in some parts of the country there are still major problems in providing high-quality in patient accommodation, often because of constraints imposed by private finance initiative (PFI) contracts entered into by predecessor authorities which bear little relationship to the current configuration of trusts
- the most apparent lack of service provision is good-quality non-hospital accommodation, which within any one locality should provide a range of levels of support and assistance to live more independently
- the new challenge of commissioning mental health services for prisons is best met by provision by general adult services, rather than from forensic services
- mapping the most common care pathways followed by service users is a useful process to monitor linkage between service elements.

Reference

1   Department of Health (2001) *Shifting the Balance of Power Within the NHS: securing delivery.* Department of Health: London.

Implementing NICE guidance: a partnership approach

Mary McClarey and Andy Dickens

Background

With an increase in the volume of NICE guidance, in the form of Health Technology Appraisals and National Clinical Guidelines, the clinical effectiveness leads of the acute and primary care trust in Plymouth came together to consider ways of making access to this information both more practical and interactive.

There was also a widely held belief that NICE guidance was not being implemented appropriately, with such parts of the service as prescribing expressing concern that NICE guidance was being 'over-implemented'. It was believed that the approved drug regime was being prescribed without giving due consideration to the parameters contained within the guidance. This needed to be addressed; not just from a financial perspective, but also to ensure that clinical governance arrangements for national guidance were robust.

In addressing these concerns, a wide range of participants from the acute trust and the PCT collaborated to form a 'Clinical Guidelines Implementation Group'. Its purpose was to agree an agenda identifying those NICE guidelines that were of the highest priority, greatest complexity and most essential to the locality. A series of workshops and satellite seminars covering the selected guidelines was subsequently arranged, providing health professionals with a forum for discussion as well as a means of dissemination to the wider community.

Attendance at the group's first meeting demonstrated a commitment within both the PCT and the acute trust at a practice level (i.e. GP, heath informatics, public heath, and clinical governance and audit). These individuals were enthusiastic, committed and gave a valuable contribution to the process. It was noted that directors from clinical and commissioning services as well as other agencies such as social services did not attend.

Group membership also included a head of department from the Institute of Health Studies, University of Plymouth, and this position was fundamental to the success of the acute trust/PCT collaboration. This academic input was engaged specifically to draw clinicians' attention to critical pieces of evidence, either due to being high graded or lacking in evidence. This took place at the beginning of the workshop and proved to be valued not just as an aid to considering the evidence but also as a guide regarding levels of evidence and guideline methodology.

The rationale for combining workshops with satellite seminars was that workshop outcomes could be disseminated to other interested health professionals. The University of Plymouth regularly broadcasts seminars to hospitals and universities across Britain using a satellite link. The broadcasts allow interaction between presenters and distant viewing sites relating to topics raised. In addition to enabling debate at the time of broadcast, the seminars are recorded and are available afterwards as both an educational and implementation tool.

NICE satellite seminars focus on theoretical *and* practical issues of guideline implementation, while the workshops are concerned with implementation alone.

Results

The trusts developed a steering group in order to identify proactively NICE guidance before its full release. The work from this group was acted on by an operational group that was responsible for arranging workshops, engaging clinical and academic experts, and ensuring appropriate representation at each workshop.

Progress to date

A total of four workshops have been held so far, addressing the following guidelines: 'orlistat, sibutramine and surgery for morbid obesity', 'pressure ulcer risk assessment and prevention', 'schizophrenia and the Health Technology Appraisal for atypical antipsychotics' and 'asthma inhaler devices for older children'.

All have been attended by relevant health professionals enabling productive discussion to take place. It was found that workshops needed to be flexible in order to access the appropriate audience, demonstrated by the asthma workshop being repeated in the evening to allow health visitors, practice nurses and GPs to attend.

Value-added result

Plymouth PCT considered that other regions would benefit from adopting a similar approach to implementing NICE guidance to that described above, and so approached the Workforce Development Confederation (WDC). This belief relates to the founding principles of NICE, in terms of reducing postcode prescribing and tackling health inequalities. It was proposed that the WDC provide the eight PCTs in the southwest peninsula with the necessary equipment to receive the satellite seminars, thus enabling clinical staff to access knowledge without leaving their workplace. The WDC approved the bid on the understanding that the availability of an on-site facility offers greater motivation to participate in debate and learning. To date, 11 sites across the peninsula have satellite-receiving equipment, shared between the eight PCTs.

Such developments demonstrate both the commitment of Plymouth teaching PCT to clinical effectiveness as well as flexible, integrated methods of learning, and the exemplary partnership between the PCT and the University of Plymouth.

Conclusion

As stated, the NICE seminars form a regular part of the satellite seminar programme broadcast by the university. In addition to this, a series of interactive health programmes has been arranged, aimed at patients and their families. The programmes address hypertension, epilepsy, diabetic foot ulcers, head injury and multiple sclerosis, and they provide the opportunity to gain more information from clinical experts as well as discuss issues with other patients.

It is evident that the approach to implementing NICE guidelines and partnership working has developed significantly. From the starting point of a local implementation group, local primary and secondary care health professionals were engaged and outcomes were disseminated to a wider audience. The work described above relied on effective partnerships between Plymouth trusts and the university, enabling debate regarding standards of care provision to take place.

A pocket guide to clinical governance

Kim Jelphs and Mike Cooke

South Staffordshire Healthcare NHS Trust was created in April 2001, formed by the merger of three culturally diverse organisations, with different models and systems for clinical governance. As an innovative, creative organisation working across a large diverse geographical area we wanted to develop something for everyone working in the organisation using a whole systems approach that would help people to:

- understand the model of clinical governance that we are developing
- be aware of what support is available and how to access it
- identify how individuals can be involved with clinical governance.

It was important to challenge the perception that clinical governance is just for clinical staff by showing how important it is for everyone to contribute to and benefit from this approach. It is not something extra or different, it is in fact 'the job'. Access to support and information is key and following consultation with staff, the *Pocket Guide* was developed (*see* Figure A).

The project

The pocket guide is a quick, portable reference guide to support all staff in using and understanding clinical governance to develop quality services and improve patient care. The guide is now in its second year and has been updated to help direct staff towards the appropriate help and support available to undertake and develop their role. The style of the guide is light, using flowcharts (*see* Figure B) as the main way of signposting information. These are grouped under the headings of 'Human resources', 'Risk management', 'Effectiveness' and 'Knowledge management', and reflect the seven pillars CHI use when assessing trusts. The contents are updated yearly to ensure information is accurate and reflects current needs (*see* Figure C).

Figure A   *A Pocket Guide to Clinical Governance.*

Part of a toolkit

Each edition has been distributed to *every* member of staff in their pay packet, supported by communication through briefings, and newsletters. An annual

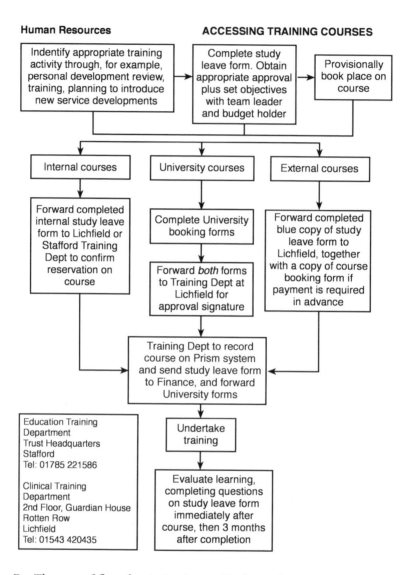

Figure B The use of flowcharts to signpost information.

week of activities to raise the profile and share learning in relation to clinical governance is also held and acts as a launch pad for the document, as we recognise it is only part of our clinical governance toolkit. Local agencies, service users, and internal and external expert speakers share learning during the week. This is known as our 'Clinical governance for real' week, which has been identified by CHI as notable practice. Colleagues joining the trust are given copies at a clinical governance induction session, and strategies, documents and reports supporting clinical governance all signpost the pocket guide. We have

INDEX

Clinical Governance and You   2

Using the Pocket Guide   3

Model of Clinical Governance in South Staffordshire Healthcare NHS Trust   4

Who's Who – Clinical Governance contacts by Directorate   5

Human Resources and Organisational Development
Communications   6
Accessing training   7
Accessing team support and development   8
Accessing mentoring support   9
Developing new ideas/raising concerns   10
Raising concerns about malpractice   11

Risk management
PALS   12
Handling complaints   13
Risk assessment   14
Critical incident   15
Health & Safety organisational signposts   16
Safe disposal of sharps   17
Drug error reporting system   18
Child protection   19

Clinical effectiveness
Accessing support for audit/quality improvement   20
Clinical benchmarking   21
Research proposals/projects   23

Knowledge management
Accessing library services   24
Caldicott Guidelines   25
Health information analysis and knowledge   26
What to do if my computer is not working   27

Useful Websites/Notes   28

Figure C

also worked with a local university as we recognised that students were finding it useful, and now it is being introduced into their training.

Language

The pocket guide breaks new ground in its simplicity, style and originality. It is a simple tool, written in language that everyone understands. It is durable and portable and definitely fits into a pocket. We have found no other tool that conveys clinical governance messages in such a succinct, accessible way, and the response and interest from other organisations and our local university concur with that view. Additionally, it is a very cost-effective way of communicating with and engaging all staff at approximately £0.50 per copy.

Outcomes

The pocket guide has definitely helped to raise the profile and understanding of clinical governance across the organisation. The CHI has identified it as notable practice; it was a key tool commented upon by our Investors in People assessor and more recently the Improving Working Lives assessment team, who all asked for copies.

Feedback from clinical and non-clinical colleagues includes:

- 'It *is* a pocket guide and easy to carry around'
- 'I use it as a memory jogger'
- 'It identifies people and where to go to for help'
- 'It reinforces things and gives us a framework to work from'
- 'The information is pertinent'.

A full academic evaluation of its impact and usefulness is being undertaken and was due for completion by December 2003.

Impact on patient care

We believe the guide has impacted upon patients and services by enabling staff to identify the help and support they need to deliver quality services for patients, service users and carers.

Sharing learning

Demonstrating transferability, 90 organisations from across the country have asked for and been sent copies of the guide, as a hard copy or a PDF file, so it can be adapted easily in their local organisations. Their feedback as part of the evaluation includes:

- 'It was shown to a meeting of frontline clinical staff and they all thought that it would really help them in their day-to-day work. Consequently the trust is now rewriting it with our own information in to be issued to all our staff (including appropriate acknowledgement)'
- 'Used as a basis for developing our own guidance'
- 'Valuable to see how other organisations approach making staff aware of

these key processes and policies. We may look at how to develop something locally'.

The guide is being reviewed in the Welsh Assembly with a view to producing something similar.

External organisations are part of the evaluation and we have evidence that it has stimulated many to develop their own versions in their organisations. It was included as part of presentations on our approach to clinical governance at the recent Human Resources and Organisational Development and British Association of Medical Managers (BAMM) national conferences. It is on the BAMM and Organisational Development Partnerships Network websites. Additionally we are delighted to have been asked to speak about the guide to the Welsh Assembly, who are interested in using it, and it has already been discussed at their clinical governance forum.

Conclusion

We recognise that the guide is just one tool that contributes to making clinical governance real in our organisation, but it is a powerful tool. It has something for everyone, has helped to raise the profile of clinical governance and its associated responsibilities in our organisation, and struck a chord with others as we all strive to take the fear out of and make clinical governance real for people.

Putting patient advocacy into practice: learning from Wales

Peter Johns

Until the end of November 2003, England and Wales shared a mechanism for involving the public and patients in NHS services. England has chosen a different route to Wales because they have decided to abolish CHCs and to develop patient and public involvement (PPI) activity in a number of different ways. The effect is to tear down existing structures and to rebuild with new ones. Wales has chosen evolution rather than revolution.

We start from CHCs. They were introduced in 1974 across England and Wales. One of their key duties at that time was hospital visiting, particularly mental hospitals, where some pretty unpleasant stories had been uncovered.

CHCs were independent bodies with a number of volunteer members drawn from local authorities, the voluntary sector and the community at large. These councils, of which 208 were established across England and Wales, were supported by a small secretariat, which was designed to convene meetings and to carry out administrative tasks. Their main duty was identified in the regulations as 'to look after the interests of the public in the NHS in that area'.

The main areas over which this was carried out included responding to consultation documents, providing general information and advice to people, hospital and clinic monitoring visits and, because no one else was doing it, helping people who had complaints against any part of the NHS to follow their complaints through the rather convoluted processes.

When Alan Milburn announced that CHCs were to be abolished, the Health and Social Services Minister at the Welsh Assembly had decided to review options for patient and public involvement and the Assembly had agreed that it wished to enhance the role of the CHCs. This rather embarrassing divergence of views was resolved by allowing in the legislation for the Welsh Assembly to have powers to keep or abolish CHCs in Wales.

Since then, the Health Wales Act has been passed, the first Welsh primary legislation since the Welsh Assembly came into being, and that formally covers the arrangements for CHCs among other things. In future, in addition to their previous core functions, CHCs will monitor all premises where NHS services are provided to patients, including GP and dental practices, private hospitals and care homes, and they will monitor the PPI activities of local health boards and trusts. They may also help them to deliver effective PPI.

This will require a statutory body to focus and manage CHC performance in Wales and this is a departure from previous practices because the statutory Board of CHCs in Wales has responsibility for allocating funding to CHCs and for ensuring that all CHCs carry out their core functions to agreed performance levels; previously all CHCs were independent and the central body acted as a mutual support organisation and all-Wales voice for CHCs.

At the same time as this is going on, CHCs are becoming more involved in 'mainstream' work. Recently, CHCs have been the external independent agency to check acute hospital baseline assessments of the hospital patient environment and their reports are presented to the trust boards and the Welsh Assembly as a recognised part of this process.

CHCs are on everyone's mailing list – we are asked for representatives to sit on a wide variety of NHS initiative groups to assist with inputting the patient's voice and we are exploring further opportunities for bringing CHC functions into the mainstream.

We cannot retain credibility, however, if we simply rely on our members' views to provide the patient's insight (although many of them have experience as patients). We gather intelligence from complaints, from monitoring visits, from anecdotal patient comments, and from surveys and focus groups. Without the facility to collect information from such a wide range of groups, we could not claim to represent patients' views.

The contrasts with England are quite striking. In England, complaints, consultations and assistance/advice to patients are carried out separately as is scrutiny of the service. How then can the patient's voice be heard effectively?

Quality improvements through nursing innovations

Jackie Dodds

Peterborough Diabetes Care Pilot, supported by the Changing Workforce Programme (CWP). Peterborough and Luton were selected as pilot sites and the project began in January 2002.

Structure

A national steering group directed the overarching project, and a local steering group was created with representatives from the whole health economy, service users and the CWP. This was supported by a project team whose role was to identify shortfalls in service, and a design team who created new roles and piloted these within the clinical areas.

Aims

Aims were to improve service to patients with:

- good quality care
- fewer 'faces' and hand offs
- enough staff to deliver care
- people with time

and to improve job satisfaction for staff giving them:

- respect and self-esteem
- job enrichment/personal growth
- variety in their work and greater flexibility.

To move this project forward would require new ways of working, increasing the breadth and depth of existing roles, and creating new roles.

Background

Diabetes is a common illness which is increasing in prevalence; approximately one person in 40 is known to have the disease, and at least another million people have it but are unaware. It is of higher incidence in Asian and black minority ethnic populations, which are highly represented in Peterborough. It is an expensive condition to manage and uses 9% of the total NHS budget. It wrecks bodies and lives.

Phase one of the pilot involved a diagnosis of current service, review pathways and considered models of care practised elsewhere. From this point it was possible to redesign the care path and design new ways of working.

The service at the inception of the project meant that 80% of type 1 diabetics were reviewed annually in hospital, 20% in the community; 10% of type 2 diabetics were reviewed in the community and 10% in hospital.

Diabetic patients have a series of clear needs:

- to establish a diagnosis
- to access appropriate medication
- lifestyle and self-management training
- screening for complications (*see* Figure A)
- treatment for complications
- care in special circumstances, e.g. pregnancy.

At the outset of the pilot, care was given by a range of healthcare professionals, hospital consultants, GPs, diabetes nurse specialists, community nurses, dieticians, podiatrists optometrists and psychologists. This represented many 'hand offs' and did not represent a good model of care in line with the patients' expressed views.

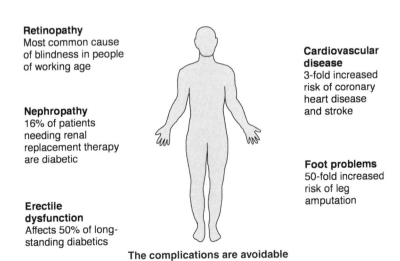

Retinopathy
Most common cause of blindness in people of working age

Nephropathy
16% of patients needing renal replacement therapy are diabetic

Erectile dysfunction
Affects 50% of long-standing diabetics

Cardiovascular disease
3-fold increased risk of coronary heart disease and stroke

Foot problems
50-fold increased risk of leg amputation

The complications are avoidable

Figure A Chronic complications of diabetes. *Source*: The Audit Commission (2000) *Testing Times. A Review of Diabetes Services in England and Wales.*

New roles piloted

Diabetes care technician

The diabetes care technician undertakes annual reviews in hospital, GP surgeries and in Boots chemist. This role has been extended to employ a further three staff. Attendance time for patients was reduced and this way of working freed up consultant time by five extra slots per clinic. Access for patients was improved by using a variety of venues.

Diabetes learning facilitators

Non-professionals from within the community trained to deliver diabetes education. This worked well as volunteers were knowledgeable about the topic and about the cultural sensitivities within the community. Group sessions were encouraged to enable a self-help network to flourish. The response from users was excellent and a business case is being drawn up to extend this service.

Senior practitioner

Diabetes specialist nurses used to only see patients specifically referred to them. Changes in treatment were sometimes delayed, as they were unable to prescribe. There were delays in transfer from sliding scale regimes due to lack of staff. There was (and still is) a lone diabetologist. This role could potentially be fulfilled by any healthcare professional working with this client group. The senior practitioner role was piloted on one ward; a diabetes nurse specialist was seconded, supported by a prescribing training course and creation of an insulin protocol. Clinical supervision was carried out by the diabetologist to give ongoing monitoring and evaluation of patient progress. The process was audited and demonstrated major improvements in practice during the period of the pilot but over-dependence on the senior practitioner by ward staff.

Conclusion

The pilot demonstrated that by taking a different approach to patterns of care delivery and traditional roles, time could be saved and the service improved. Continual development and multiskilling into these roles will continue, in order to address the increasing service need from within finite resources.

Phase 2 Cardiac Rehabilitation Pilot Programme: Leeds North West PCT

Sue Kendal

After a heart attack or heart surgery, patients are uncertain and anxious about their future. Unfortunately immediately post-hospital discharge (this period of time is referred to as phase 2) heart patients often experience minimal support. This period of time may be particularly important, however, in terms of both supporting the transition back to wellbeing and in establishing the lifestyle changes that impact on future cardiac health. During this period of time – post-hospital discharge and prior to attendance at phase 3 exercise and health education programme – patients tend to suffer from 'homecoming anxiety' and are often left to fend for themselves. The aim of the Leeds North West phase 2 Cardiac Rehabilitation Pilot Programme is to address this deficit.

It was considered that local support through primary care is where support at this time should logically be provided. The primary care team often has previous knowledge of and existing relationships with the patient, and they are ideally placed to provide ongoing care. Furthermore, the services are locally accessible and familiar to the patients and their relatives. We set out to develop this service and in doing so met with the traditional boundaries and barriers between primary and secondary care.

Primary and secondary care services have historically worked separately, in isolation, yet the patient travels between both. The patients' experience of care can often feel disjointed. Our programme aimed to address this issue so that the patient's experience is of a 'joined-up' service where their needs are met by local and hospital services working in harmony. Ultimately, our vision is that the patient need not be concerned whether a service is based in a primary care setting or an acute hospital, but sees only that support is available at the right time and at the right place to meet their needs.

We set out to create a seamless care pathway where the strengths of both primary and secondary care can be utilised to the full. To achieve this we proposed that the discharge of patients following myocardial infarction and coronary artery bypass surgery was made in nursing terms, directly from the rehabilitation team to the lead coronary heart disease (CHD) practice nurses in general practices.

This would facilitate a 30-minute phase 2 review appointment within primary care to be offered within the first two weeks after discharge, and addressing issues which are important within phase 2 of the Cardiac Rehabilitation Programme.

The phase 2 cardiac rehabilitation appointment aims to:

- empower the patient to make lifestyle changes to reduce some and eliminate other risk factors
- further increase the knowledge of their condition gained as an inpatient and address cardiac misconceptions
- enable the patient to resume their daily activities with confidence
- assist the patients and their partners to attain psychological wellbeing
- assist the patient to return to their employment where appropriate
- promote adherence to secondary prevention medication
- provide a review of patients' symptoms, clinical measurements and general recovery
- provide information on phase 3 rehabilitation and encourage attendance.

The interaction is patient centred and involves carers. It is supported by the use of a computerised CHD template (which aids data collection and audit) and a clinical practice guideline. The exact content of the appointment depends on the specific needs of the patient and their problems. Follow-up appointments are arranged as appropriate. At all times the CHD-trained practice nurses in primary care have an option to refer to the hospital cardiac rehabilitation team for advice when needed.

At present we have nine practices whose nurses are involved in the phase 2 pilot programme.

The project proposals are:

- on discharge, a member of the cardiac rehabilitation nursing team rings and makes appointments on behalf of the patients with the named CHD-trained practice nurse and informs the patient of the appointment details
- the appointment is for 30 minutes and occurs within two weeks of discharge
- a discharge proforma is sent directly to the practice nurse, by post, with information about lifestyle and rehabilitation work initiated in hospital
- patients are issued with a personal cardiac health record – a patient-held record that aids communication
- communication of any relevant information back to the rehabilitation team prior to phase 3 is positively encouraged.

It is hoped that this system of care will influence the uptake of phase 3 rehabilitation yet be flexible to respond to patients who are not wanting or unable to attend a phase 3 group.

The pilot programme activity levels are being evaluated, together with an overview of the patient characteristics, referral patterns and attendance data. The programme is also audited using patient feedback questionnaires and reflection on practice questionnaires that are completed by the CHD-trained practice nurses.

The programme is currently in its pilot stage and preliminary results are already proving it to be successful. It is hoped that this area of good practice will be shared with other interested parties and be developed further to encompass more patients and increase the numbers who would hopefully benefit from such interaction.

Action on ENT: Blackburn's experience

Sarah Fitch

Reason for change

Blackburn Royal Infirmary (BRI) serves a highly deprived community of mixed minorities. Access to healthcare is of concern because of the language barriers and the greater needs in actual healthcare. Long waiting lists for outpatient consultations and for surgery create an agonising situation both for the community and the healthcare workers.

The Ear, Nose and Throat (ENT) Department at BRI, with just a small amount of time and finance gained from *Action on ENT* has enabled a major change to take place in the provision of healthcare in ENT.

Ideas

Most healthcare workers have plenty of ideas for schemes which they know would improve services for patients. But because of lack of time, low budget and lack of a forum to discuss these ideas, services remain bogged down in bureaucracy and lack of initiative. *Action on ENT* was our forum to thrash out and further discuss these ideas with others. Key to the change in services was the composition of our group: two clinicians with a keen interest in change for a more modern way of providing services; nursing and audiology staff keen to take on new enhanced roles and responsibilities; and of course management to help implement change, monitor progress and keep account of the budget. All staff were equally important, each with an opinion worth sharing, considering and implementing.

The extended role of the nurse

If one follows the Pareto principle, 80% of conditions that flow through a clinic can be managed by nursing staff who have been trained and follow protocols for management of these categories of ailment. Protocols drawn up in the form of questionnaires and flowcharts can be used to guide the way the patient is managed and also form a means of auditing the work being carried out and the results being achieved. In our department there are several areas where our specialist nurse practitioner has taken a lead.

Postoperative telephone follow-up of the patient who has undergone nasal surgery

Patients undergoing postoperative follow-up after nasal surgery form a large proportion of the patients seen in the clinic. Our 'three-day challenge' was to stop seeing these patients so that the capacity would increase immediately. Most patients are satisfied with the results of their nasal surgery. Patients who are concerned about their condition after surgery tend to ring the clinic and make an earlier appointment than their routine three-month follow-up. So are routine follow-up appointments really necessary?

A PDSA cycle was implemented. The stages of the cycle were:

1   stopped making appointments for postnasal surgery patients for two consultants
2   concerns raised by clinicians at other *Action on ENT* sites
3   decision to follow up these patients by telephone call from the specialist nurse practitioner at three months
4   protocol questionnaire created for formalised phone call.

Results

Over a nine-month period for two consultants:

- 167 patients were processed
- 136 were happy and discharged (89%)
- 17 required clinic appointment (10%) (they received a booked appointment)
- 150 outpatient slots were released.

This also reduced the steps in the patient pathway for nasal surgery.

Listing of patients for tonsillectomy

Anecdotal evidence again suggests that by the time the patient is seen in clinic, the decision to go ahead with tonsillectomy has already been made either by the family doctor or the patient themselves. A routine visit to a consultant clinic is not necessary except to explain the procedure and to exclude the few patients who have been referred inappropriately.

A process map of the patient with recurrent tonsillitis revealed multiple visits to hospital were taking place: first for the initial consultation, second for pre-assessment and finally for the operation. Our plan was for the patient to be seen and considered for listing by the specialist nurse practitioner. Once a decision to list the patient had been made, they also underwent pre-anaesthetic assessment by the specialist nurse practitioner. Our department sees approximately 600 patients for tonsillectomy every year. A PDSA cycle was set up as follows:

1 protocol set in the form of a questionnaire
2 approval by all consultants
3 specialist nurse practitioner-led clinic introduced with nurse pre-assessment and listing
4 patient placed on pooled waiting list
5 six or seven patients seen in independent clinic held once a week
6 rapid two-week access made available for patients with unexpected problems
7 implementation of two clinics per week
8 plan made to extend service to peripheral units
9 nurse consent a problem – trust discussions under way, also awaiting Royal College of Nursing (RCN) guidelines.

Results

Over a nine-month period:

- 276 patients were processed
- 245 were listed (89%)
- 21 were rejected (8%)
- 6 saw a consultant
- 251 new patient slots were released.

Access times were previously a 14–15-week outpatient wait, then 4–5 months on a waiting list, giving a total wait of about 130 days. The current wait from referral to treatment is now 67.5 days

Aural care clinic

Our figures show that 966 outpatient appointments are made for routine review and cleaning of mastoid cavities in consultant clinics and 200 patients attend outpatients with otitis externa. PDSA cycle stages included:

1 specialist nurse practitioner requested to go on aural care training course at another unit
2 specialist nurse practitioner not trained in use of microscope on the course
3 in-house training commenced for outpatient nursing and audiology staff in all aspects of aural care
4 clinics performed with consultant input
5 independent clinics with fast access available for problem patients to five consultant clinics (within two weeks)
6 patients can ring directly and book appointments
7 plans to extend aural care training to the North West region on twice-yearly courses.

Results

To date 583 outpatient appointments have been saved or 1166 follow-up slots.

The extended role of the audiologist

Having studied process maps of patients going through our department we found that the work done to see a paediatric patient following grommet insertion was being duplicated. The children were having their ears examined twice, by the consultant and the audiologist. The 'efficient' time spent was with the audiologist, averaging 20 minutes.

The children were spending on average over 90 minutes to go through the process of attending a clinic for a check-up. Shockingly, on average they were spending two minutes only with the clinician, during that visit. Most of their time was wasted sitting waiting to see the consultant.

An urgent need to change the service for this group of patients was required. A PDSA cycle had already commenced with the process map. Stages of change involved the following:

1 protocol for follow-up in the form of a questionnaire drawn up
2 protocol agreed with all consultants in the unit
3 solo 'audiology' follow-up clinic conducted with consultant in attendance to monitor progress for each senior audiologist doing the clinic
4 audiologists do clinic on their own within normal working hours
5 clinics held out of hours (1700–1900) as this involves less disruption to ordinary consultant clinics and is more patient friendly
6 service extended to under-three-year-olds, therefore visual response audiometry equipment purchased
7 service extended to community audiology service.

Results

To date:

- 104 routine follow-up patients have been seen by an audiologist
- 27 required a consultant opinion
- 10 were discharged
- 39 did not attend (inherited from the previous system – now moved to partial booking)
- 12 were transferred
- there is an anticipated saving of 750 follow-up visits per year.

Clinics are held in the evening and patient satisfaction surveys have been very favourable.

Process maps

In our ignorance we accept that we are providing an 'efficient' service for our patients. Without looking at how patients are actually treated it is difficult to know what processes are a waste of time, both for the patient and the health-care worker. We studied the patient's journey from the GP letter arriving in the hospital post to being seen by the clinician and an appointment sent for the patient, right up to the patient's treatment and discharge. Shocking wastes and inefficiencies were identified. This should be the beginning of change.

Capacity and demand measures

Measuring clinical activity is vital. It forms the basis for change. How many patients are being referred on average? Therefore, how many patients need to be seen at each clinic to maintain waiting times at a minimum? Statistics such as these are powerful tools for setting resource levels.

Waiting list times for outpatients and theatres

Patient access measured as waiting times is a good method of monitoring change from improvement in services. Our access times have changed from an average of 13 weeks to eight weeks with no patients waiting longer than 13 weeks for an outpatient appointment. All surgery is now performed within six months and for the two consultants leading the modernisation work, all surgery is now carried out in less than three months. Clinics now routinely end on time (though we never thought of collecting this data). Clinic slots have been increased to allow a longer time with each patient; numbers have been reduced from 18 down to 13 patients per clinic session for each doctor. All our staff report feeling that clinics offer a higher quality of service to patients and reduced levels of stress for all involved.

Conclusion

For the period May 2001 to May 2002, by examining current practice and developing the role of the specialist nurse practitioner and the audiology role, the department of ENT at BRI has managed to release 1423 outpatient slots. This has allowed improved access to around eight weeks for outpatients and less than three months for surgery. It has also enabled clinics to become more manageable and individual consultants' time with patients to be increased.

Multidisciplinary teams working together here have demonstrated the real benefits that can be effected.

Facing up to failure: the impact of the star ratings

Jeremy Berger and Phil Glanfield

Context

Government policy is based on setting standards and targets for health services against which organisations are measured, reviewed and inspected. From time to time there are well-publicised 'system failures' in health services which result in enquiries, reports and remedial action. Around publication date we hear a lot about star ratings, particularly zero-star or 'failing' organisations, but what happens when the publicity has died down? What is it like to work in a zero-star trust? How do patients react, does it make a difference?

Case study

In 2000/2001 Barnet and Chase Farm Hospitals Trust missed its key targets and therefore had no stars in September 2001. In January 2002 it was subject to a clinical governance review by the CHI, published in March 2002. The review score was such that they had no stars in July 2002. In the course of the CHI review it came to light that 2700 general ultrasound requests had not been given appointments. A similar incident had occurred in April 2000, which the trust had dealt with. CHI announced the launch of an enquiry in February 2002 and the report was published in November 2002. The trust chair and chief executive resigned and the trust was 'franchised' to a new chief executive. The trust was awarded one star in July 2003.

The Performance Development Trust (PDT) is part of the NHS Modernisation Agency. Its brief is to help and support zero-star trusts to regain a star and to improve the experience for patients, staff and stakeholders. The PDT has recently completed a range of work with Barnet and Chase Farm, including support to the radiology directorate.

Ratings: policy and practice

The whole approach to targets and ratings has attracted debate and contro-versy. Recent reports from the Public Administration Select Committee, the

Royal Statistical Society, the Audit Commission and last year's Reith Lectures highlight the limitations and potential counterproductive effects of targets – as well as potential benefits if managed well.[1-4] The field is rife with paradoxes and contradictions, such as:

- it is good to have few targets to provide focus and local discretion and it is necessary to consider a wide range of indicators to assess quality
- a national service should work to national standards ('no postcode lottery') and standards are most likely to be achieved when developed by the front line but this takes time and is likely to be contested.

PDT experience is that star ratings create their own dynamic. A zero-star rating can be a 'wake-up call' and, at the same time, demoralise staff and be used as a stick to beat the trust. There are a number of stories of patients remarking 'I suppose that is what you get from a zero-star trust'. Given that the consequences of a zero rating are so significant, we need to be confident that the assessment system is accurate and reliable. CHAI (and others) have acknowledged that we have some way to go in this regard.

Intervention: emerging evidence, theory and practice

Intervening to improve performance seems to be an inevitable consequence of performance rating and inspection systems. If an institution is to be 'named and shamed' as providing a substandard service, then those that are served will expect 'something to be done'. This is a relatively new approach to the management of public services and most of the available research focuses on commerce, where the context is different. Intervention is often prompted by the company's bankers and focused on cost reduction (production and product range) and financial restructuring. This is likely to result in a reduction in sales (and an even greater reduction in cost of sales) but reducing activity is not likely to be available to a public service. However, there are also important similarities that seem to hold good for the public sector. The evidence suggests that three broad strands of intervention are necessary:

- *replacement*: getting the right people in the right place. Typically in the commercial sector a chief executive will be left in post because of their relationship with customers, and the intervention team will focus on finance and operations. In the NHS there are often changes at the top of organisations associated with star ratings. In addition the PDT experience suggests that leadership and management is often missing from the 'middle' of the organisation – clinical directors and directorate or business managers. Strengthening leadership and management is critical for recovery
- *retrenchment*: just as controlling production and the cost of sales is critical in

business, so controlling the patient pathway (referrals, waiting times and lists, risk, audit, bed and discharge management) are critical in healthcare. In 2003, most acute trusts with a zero-star rating failed to hit their financial target

- *renewal*: there is a danger that short-term expediency dominates the recovery process, but 'target chasing' is not sustainable and can be counter-productive. The engagement of patients, staff (particularly clinical) and partners is essential. The PDT has found that some zero-rated trusts are highly fragmented, where consultants 'do their own thing', and patient pathways or protocols are not shared across primary and secondary care or even between consultants. The financial crisis is regarded as 'management's problem', not related to activity. The social and intellectual capacity of an organisation is hard to measure but we know that in high-performing organisations everyone takes an interest in the whole as well as their part; when there is a problem people rally around, teamwork is everywhere, there is a clear, local sense of direction, services are focused around the patient not the target, and performance exceeds the target. Staff are curious, questioning, never satisfied with their service and are well connected to others with a common interest.[5]

References

1   Select Committee on Public Administration, 27 February 2003. www.parliament.the-stationery-office.co.uk

2   Royal Statistical Society Working Party on Performance Monitoring in the Public Services (2003) *Performance Indicators: good, bad and ugly.* www.rss.org.uk

3   Audit Commission (2003) *Targets in the Public Sector.* Audit Commission: London. www.auditcommission.gov.uk

4   O'Neill O (2002) *A Question of Trust.* Reith Lectures. www.bbc.co.uk/radio4

5   Glanfield PJ (2003) Towards sustainable change and improvement. In: S Pickering and J Thompson (eds) *Clinical Governance and Best Value.* Churchill Livingstone: London.

The Commission for Health Improvement: putting recommendations into practice

Paul Bates

The challenges of putting recommendations into practice following a CHI inspection are directly related to the extent to which the PCT has influenced those recommendations.

Herefordshire PCT was selected as one of eight PCTs in the first wave of CHI PCT reviews.

From the outset, expectations of the CHI review process were very high. The extent to which these expectations were met was a factor in the resultant climate in which the report was received and acted upon.

Key elements of the learning from the pilot included:

- making sure that the organisation and its stakeholders clearly understood the purpose of a CHI review
- understanding that what comes out of a CHI review is very largely dependent on what the organisation puts into the review. It should not be a passive and reactive process
- helping the CHI and its reviewers to understand the nature of the organisation
- creating an atmosphere in which the organisation welcomed the CHI review as an opportunity to look into the mirror and see whether the organisation was indeed as handsome as it thought it was
- shaking the organisation out of any complacency by making it clear that CHI reviewers would be more interested in the experiences of patients than the quality of the prose in a clinical governance report
- helping the CHI team, including taking measures to make their working week easier, which were the actions of a sensible organisation wanting to be reviewed by friendly critics
- being prepared and having the stamina for a process which takes many months from start to finish
- being ready to comment on the draft report and reach agreement with the

CHI on changes that are necessary to ensure the report is accurate and of the maximum use.

The report painted a very positive picture of the organisation, but did not meet all its expectations. For many it did not fulfil their expectation that they were among the best in their profession, and for some it was a disappointment that their particular department was not mentioned at all. GPs were particularly disappointed not to receive feedback to individual practices which had been visited by CHI reviewers. In many respects, the organisation failed to keep the right perspective on the process.

Putting the recommendations into practice required the organisation and its broader stakeholders to take ownership of them. We were aware of some organisations that had put the minimal amount of effort into the action-planning day, at which CHI recommendations are meant to be understood, tested and converted into specific action plans. Our significant investment in that day was rewarded with an incredibly positive response from a broad range of stakeholders, including the public, who helped shape the action plans.

On receipt of the final report, the PCT had been able to acknowledge to CHI that it was able to recognise itself from the observations and recommendations in the report. The recommendations varied from those that were constructive and incisive to those that seemed either irrelevant or peripheral.

The time span over which recommendations are put into practice depends largely on their content. Those that require strategic investment or reshaping of services can take months if not years to achieve. Those that highlight imminent risks to patients will need immediate action. The key areas for action highlighted by the commission were to:

- work with our local acute trust and other partners to resolve the problems in coping with emergency admissions and to reduce the extent to which patients awaiting admission are 'stacked' at home
- improve communication systems with staff and in particular to clarify roles and responsibilities of management and senior staff
- improve the engagement of allied health professionals in the planning and delivery of services
- review and take action on the workload of locality managers
- further disseminate risk management systems into primary care
- further implement Caldicott recommendations
- put in place a robust information technology and management (IM&T) strategy.

There is no doubt at all that in highlighting our health economy difficulties in coping with admissions and our need to improve information and IT the CHI had highlighted two of the biggest challenges facing the health system. Indeed, had they not highlighted these we would have questioned whether the process had been undertaken successfully. Other recommendations were more curious.

The action in relation to the involvement of allied health professionals seemed to reflect the personal interests and professional backgrounds of some of the review team members and the bond they developed with some of their peers in the trust. The recommendation that the trust should examine the workload of its managers seemed to turn on its head years of pressure to reduce management costs.

While the trust must address these recommendations, not least if it is to satisfy its SHA that it has given the appropriate priority to the CHI review, in practice it must incorporate the recommendations into the trust's own strategic, service and organisational development plans if they are to be implemented in a logical and coherent way which ensures they are sustainable.

The Herefordshire experience is based on a pilot process where, inevitably, the latitude applied by both the CHI review team and the trust was greater than it would be now that the CHI has significantly more experience of the process. The advent of star ratings for PCTs has changed the PCT's perspective of the CHI and the review, and the star ratings are now seen as absolutely fundamental to the development, reputation and credibility of the organisation. Herefordshire is a three-star trust and is determined to remain so. In order to do so it will need to incorporate star-rating indicators into its mainstream performance management systems and it must be prepared to apply its own learning from the pilot review in preparing for the next review, which is approaching all too fast, and will without doubt be more demanding than the pilot.

The implementation of NICE Technology Appraisal Guidance within a cancer centre

Diana Mort, Carol Jordan and Gill Williams

Introduction

Over the past three years NICE has published 68 technology appraisals and 13 clinical guideline programmes. The implementation of this guidance poses enormous challenges for the NHS, affecting service delivery, resource allocation, clinical audit and clinical governance.

Implementation framework

Cancer services is one of the five divisions within Velindre NHS Trust, Cardiff. The clinical governance manager of the trust receives all NICE Technology Appraisal Guidance (NICE TAG). The publications that are relevant to an oncology service are identified and highlighted to the cancer services manager, who circulates the documentation to appropriate personnel within the division. Fifteen multidisciplinary clinical process teams (CPTs) have been set up within cancer services – nine are tumour site-specific (breast, colorectal, upper gastro-intestinal, lung, gynaecological, urological, head and neck, brain and lymphoma) and six are service-specific (outpatients, inpatients, radiotherapy, chemotherapy, palliative care and diagnostic imaging). Each team discusses NICE guidance relevant to their area of work. A local opinion is agreed and an implementation strategy outlined. Routine clinical audits on adherence to guidance are developed and the results reported to the Cancer Services Clinical Governance Committee on an annual basis.

NICE guidance relevant to cancer services

The 17 NICE TAG publications relevant to an oncology service have been discussed by the appropriate CPT. The division has looked at the use of taxanes, trastuzumab, vinorelbine and capecitabine in breast cancer; taxanes, topotecan and liposomal doxorubicin in ovarian cancer; irinotecan, oxaliplatin, raltitrexed and capecitabine in colorectal cancer; gemcitabine in pancreatic cancer; temazolamide in high-grade gliomas; rituximab in lymphoma, and taxanes and gemcitabine in lung cancer. Other areas reviewed were ultrasound-guided insertion of central venous lines and computerised cognitive behaviour therapy for anxiety and depression.

Opinion of local CPT

Following review and detailed discussion on the local implications of each NICE TAG by the specific CPT, a local consensus of opinion was formed. In most cases identical local protocols were already in place (3.6.23.28.30.45.54.55) and so there was no need for change in current management policies. In other cases new local protocols were agreed following NICE guidance (25.34.61.62) or business cases were written (49.51) in order to implement new developments. It was felt there was insufficient evidence in the NICE TAG to change the local management plan in two areas (26.37) and a further paper (33) underwent minimal adjustment before being accepted locally. Reasons to justify the above actions were clearly reported to the Clinical Governance Committee.

Funding

The local health boards have provided funding to cover the costs of all NICE-approved drugs. However, the service implications in terms of increases in staff numbers or loss of trust income when changing from intravenous to oral chemotherapy have not been covered. Separate business cases have been written and submitted under the service and financial framework process.

Clinical audits

Problems were encountered in developing robust clinical audit tools. Many NICE TAG papers suggest that a particular treatment should be considered in a subset of patients. Audits on whether a drug has been used appropriately have been relatively easy to devise, but audits on whether the technology has been considered in the whole subset of patients are far more extensive and the data have not been available.

Velindre NHS Trust Cancer Services uses an electronic patient record with a core clinical minimum dataset recorded on all patients referred to the division. Analysis of this dataset enabled us to identify particular subsets of patients for audits on adherence to NICE guidance. However, additional data were required with regard to patient performance status, clinical trial entry, whether chemotherapy was first-, second- or third-line and sites of metastatic disease. In order to facilitate clinical audit on adherence to NICE guidance, three new audit methodologies were considered – the use of a new consent to treatment form; new chemotherapy prescription sheets; and expansion of the patient management plan to include a statement on NICE guidance.

Consent form audit

In April 2003, our patient consent to treatment form was revised in accordance with guidance from the Welsh Assembly. In addition to the advised changes we incorporated questions on adherence to NICE guidance. An audit on completion of the new consent forms was undertaken. The medical records of patients commencing radiotherapy or chemotherapy (90 sets) were examined. A signed consent form was filed in the notes in 87 cases, and the new consent form was used in 81 patients. The section on adherence to NICE guidance was completed on 60/81 forms. There was no NICE guidance available on at least 42 treatments given. In 16/18 remaining cases, treatment was given in accordance with NICE TAG and there were clinical reasons for non-compliance in two cases.

This audit methodology was not successful. The inclusion of questions regarding NICE guidance on our standard consent form resulted in increased time to obtain patient consent and was inappropriate for the majority of treatments given, where no NICE guidance is available. The audit was time consuming as the medical records had to be hand-searched for the consent form. The use of chemotherapy prescription sheets to collate these data, with prospective entry on to the electronic patient record, is under consideration.

Clinical governance

The stage of review, implementation, monitoring and reporting on NICE TAG within our trust is recorded on our clinical effectiveness/audit intranet page.

Seventeen NICE TAGs have been discussed within Cancer Services, Velindre NHS Trust, and a policy to implement the guidance agreed in 15/17 cases. Business cases have been written for more resources in order to implement the guidance on computerised cognitive behavioural therapy and ultrasound-guided placement of central venous lines. The other 13 TAGs have been implemented. Formal audits have demonstrated complete adherence to the guidance on taxanes in breast and ovarian cancer, and gemcitabine in pancreatic cancer, and partial adherence to guidance on palliative chemotherapy for colorectal cancer, temazolamide for high-grade gliomas and rituximab for lymphoma.

Conclusions

Reporting on the implementation of NICE guidance is a standard requirement in the annual clinical governance reports from each of our clinical process teams. This has generated more work in terms of policy writing, service development, clinical audit and reporting. Funding for some areas of development is still awaited. The NICE guidance has facilitated the development of consensus opinion on management policies within the trust and enabled us to obtain additional funding for new drugs.

2003 audit of NICE guidelines for the use of electronic fetal monitoring at the Princess Anne Hospital, Southampton University Hospitals NHS Trust

Sucheta Iyengar, Patricia Norman, Suzanne Cunningham and Matthew Coleman

- An interprofessional approach to auditing the recent NICE electronic fetal monitoring (EFM) guidelines has had many positive spin-offs. It has increased multidisciplinary awareness and understanding of each other's roles and supported significant changes in practice.
- The process of auditing improved staff awareness of standards – some of the standards in the guideline were new to staff.
- Auditing has stimulated appropriate use of NICE EFM standards for all women.
- The NICE guidelines for EFM are comprehensive and required at least seven separate audits.
- Notable success also included a substantial reduction in the use of inappropriate EFM and the replacement of ten older EFM monitors. The successful bid for monies to replace them was influenced by clinicians and substantiated by the standards in the guideline for EFM.

Methods

In May 2001 NICE issued *Clinical Guideline C: the use of electronic fetal monitoring.* It was an inherited guideline. At the beginning of 2003, the Princess Anne Hospital's maternity services decided to audit the guideline. Audit meetings were multidisciplinary, and included midwives, a risk manager, a representative from the clinical effectiveness team, a consultant in fetal medicine and a member of the junior medical staff.

Immediate progress was established by using the algorithm at the centre of the guideline to produce an audit tool that contained variances for all eventualities on the algorithm. The audit tool was then split into two areas – those applicable to midwifery and those applicable to medical staff. At this point each of the disciplines concentrated on auditing their own areas, but reported findings to a multidisciplinary meeting.

At the point of submission of the abstract for presentation to the NICE 2003 conference, six 'bite-size' audits had taken place:

1 intermittent auscultation in low-risk women
2 EFM: women's perceptions
3 EFM practice issues, including audit of equipment and training
4 key outcome measures
5 fetal blood sampling (FBS): case notes
6 FBS: self-audit of staff awareness of NICE guideline.

Results

The following are 'some of' and by no means 'all' the results. For more detailed information about the audits email: patricia.norman@suht.swest.nhs.uk

Intermittent auscultation in low-risk women

This was a prospective audit of women's notes and case midwives' experience (36 low risk and 2 moderate risk)

Standard: intermittent auscultation (IA) during the first stage of labour should take place every 15 minutes

Figure A shows the percentage of women who had IA every 15 minutes during the 1st stage of labour. Reasons given for not having IA in the 1st stage were:

- it was not thought to be appropriate by midwife (2/38)
- the midwife otherwise occupied (6/38)
- the risk assessment changed (2/38).

After review, variances from the standard were all considered to be for clinically sound reasons.

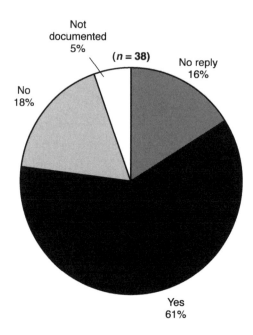

Figure A The percentage of women who had IA every 15 minutes during the 1st stage of labour.

Standard: IA in the second stage of labour should be performed and documented at least every five minutes

The results for this procedure were found to be:

- yes 66% (25/38)
- no 8% (3/38)
- no reply 26% (10/38).

Reasons given for IA not being undertaken every five minutes during the second stage were (*n*):

- it was not thought to be appropriate by midwife (4)
- the risk assessment changed (2)
- there was a very quick delivery (1)
- it was done more frequently (2).

After review, variances from the standard were all considered to be for clinically sound reasons.

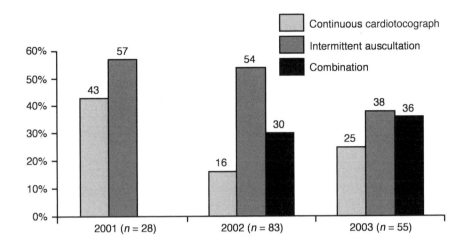

Figure B   The change of practice in fetal heart rate monitoring over three years.

Fetal heart rate monitoring during the first stage of labour

Figure B shows the change in practice and culture over a three-year period. By 2003 the number of women having EFM had reduced by almost half. The category 'combination' was used from 2002 because the audit results of 2001 revealed that some women were on IA in the early stages of labour and sometimes had continuous monitoring at the final stage.

EFM: women's perceptions

This important audit was designed to involve the women and used a sample of ten women. It was distributed on the wards by the midwife caring for the woman. We suspected that time constraints at the time of auditing caused a low response rate. The audit tool will be improved for a re-audit planned in the near future. In addition, the time period over which the audit is conducted will be extended with the hope of increasing the sample size to at least 25.

The results were as follows:

- 8 had the opportunity, while pregnant, to discuss fetal monitoring
- 9 received an explanation from a midwife or doctor of the benefits of continuous monitoring
- 7 women felt they were kept informed regularly about baby's heart beat during labour
- 2 felt they weren't informed enough.

EFM practice issues: education and equipment

The standard here was that for EFM, any member of staff who is asked to provide an opinion on a trace should note their findings on both the trace and maternal case notes along with the date, time and signature.

A snapshot concurrent audit of 11 case notes took place; 3/11 required an opinion. Of these three:

1   there was no trace matching the time in labour notes
2   there was a trace with a date and opinion (satisfied), no time was recorded
3   there was a trace with a date and time but no opinion.

A solution that is being tried is to use a sticky label to record EFM interpretation.

EFM monitors

There are 12 EFM monitors on the labour ward, five on the high-risk ward, two on the low-risk unit. All machines are 15–20 years old and ten are obsolete. A bid has been accepted for ten replacements costing £53 586.96 excluding VAT – they have been ordered. The new machines have the capacity to take archiving software at a later date when monies become available. Also, two machines are equipped with telemetry to enable improved mobility in labour. Currently the standard for archiving the EFM traces is difficult to achieve, primarily because of the quality of the trace paper. Traces are stored in brown envelopes for added protection, but it is recognised that this is substandard and there are many instances where this filing system fails.

Settings on the monitors are standard and they are serviced annually. Occasionally when batteries are renewed they may be incorrectly reset but this is instantly obvious to health professionals because the graph paper alters in appearance. Changing the batteries can also affect the time settings on the clock. A solution to this would be for one person, who is trained in adjusting the settings, to change batteries on all the machines regularly.

Staff training on EFM monitors

- There is an annual mandatory and K2 training system: there was a 49% attendance rate September 2002–September 2003.
- K2 software for EFM training is generally used by the same staff that attended the mandatory training. There may be an issue with midwifery IT skills, and it is recognised that limited time is a major constraint. *Note*: since this audit it has come to light that the K2 software has failed to record all hits; therefore, the figure of 49% is likely to have been higher.

Key outcome measures

Evidence of all outcome measures in guideline (2.8) is collected on the hospital integrated clinical support system (HICSS) except:

- cerebral palsy and neurodevelopmental disability – this data is collected by the community child health team
- neonatal encephalopathy: this will be on the new HICSS neonatal system which is in a pilot stage.

The compliance for collecting key outcome measures is 100%. However, some of the outcomes are not forwarded to any other organisation within the NHS, and there is significant confusion about the final destination and purpose of these outcomes. Contact has been made with the health authority to inform them of the information that is now available from HICSS.

Fetal blood sampling (FBS): case notes

This was a retrospective study of 30 case notes (all identified from the electronic maternity database – HICSS).

Sample

The sample consisted of all women undergoing fetal blood sampling between November 2002 and February 2003. All notes were reviewed by a single observer. EFM was confirmed as pathological in *all* case notes (i.e. FBS was considered appropriate).

Results

- Documentation of NICE-recommended immediate measures:
  - left lateral position   50% (15)
  - crystalline infusion   7% (2)
  - syntocinon reduced or stopped   10% (3)

- When FBS was normal (pH ≥ 7.25) in   86% (26)
  - FBS not repeated in   53% (16)
  - FBS repeated in   23% (7)
  - technical failure   10% (3)

- Post-delivery paired cord gases recorded in   90% (27)
  - 2 were only venous
  - 1 was not documented

- Apgar scores documented after birth in all   100%

FBS: self-audit of staff awareness of NICE guideline

The aim was to produce an educational audit tool for staff to use to assess their own understanding of FBS, and increase awareness of NICE guidelines relating to FBS.

Sample

The sample included all medical and senior midwifery staff who might be involved in the management and interpretation of FBS. Sample size = 31, with 100% response rate.

Results

- Awareness of reasons for recommending EFM was > 90% except in the categories:
  - maternal choice
  - midwifery choice.
- Awareness that any unit employing EFM should have access to FBS facilities was 84% (25).
- Awareness of most aspects of the guideline (including immediate measures for fetal bradycardia, but incomplete documentation) was > 90%.
- Awareness of measures to be taken with various pH values was 97%.
- Audit of local procedures (i.e use of FBS machine and capillary tubes): awareness of various procedures associated with capillary tubes ranged from 61 to 87%.
- Comments highlighted technical difficulties with the analyser. These will be dealt with locally.

Actions

- Teams are working on audit actions.
- A comprehensive audit of EFM traces and documentation is planned for November 2003.
- The study highlighted the benefits of self-audit: this will be repeated.
- A strategy for updating staff on EFM is now being developed.
- A more comprehensive audit of women's views will be carried out.
- A re-audit will be conducted.

Conclusion

This 'bite-size' approach to auditing NICE guidelines was highly successful and clinically effective in Southampton. The specific audit findings have been outlined in this chapter. The other positive aspects include increased enthusiasm for audit and its benefits and a better realisation of the gap between best and actual practice.

Developing your skills and enhancing your career

John Whitmore

Change is the only constant. While we may yearn for personal stability, many irresistible and apparently diverse forces (consumer expectations, political decisions, global insecurity, economic blips, legislative change and pharmacological advances, to name but a few) contrive to shape current and future healthcare delivery. While you may personally yearn for stability and apparent security in this sea of change, others approach the challenges of adapting differently. They recognise that they are largely unable to control the unpredictable nature of their environment. They also recognise that they always have one fundamental choice – the choice of how they respond to changing circumstances. This choice is available to all of us, and recognising it allows us to gain control over our lives. A coaching style of leadership adopts the principle of choice and in doing so unlocks individual and collective potential for change.

The challenges that face the NHS are many. At a personal level my family members have experienced high levels of care from the NHS. However, I recognise that the NHS, like all organisations, cannot isolate itself from the world that it inhabits. The NHS, and you as a member of it, have choices about how to respond to current changes – passive resistance, active resistance or compliance to name a few. *The NHS Plan* describes the challenges faced by the NHS and outlines how these challenges will be addressed. However, we all know that the production of a vision, a plan for the future, in an organisation as complex as the NHS, does not in itself bring it about. And the very act of describing the future begins to remove choice and control for individuals, teams and organisations.

This is where a coaching leader can bring about sustainable changes in healthcare delivery. Inspiring a single individual to change, to behave differently, can prove extremely difficult. You may care to reflect on your experiences of patient compliance. Consider the task of change in a large, complex organisation steeped in cultures of professionalism, hierarchy and control; consider the challenge of change in the NHS. A 'telling' style limits the choices that your average highly educated NHS adult has, and is unlikely to lead to long-term sustainable change. It will, over time, erode commitment and contribution. You may be thinking that the NHS is currently doing this to others and to me. However, we all need to recognise our own place in the 'system' and the way in which we as leaders behave. Taking this responsibility requires self-belief and self-awareness.

Individuals, teams and organisations can and do change; this change, however, is often not driven by dictate and imposition but via the effective engagement of individuals and teams. By this I mean engagement of their hands, heads and hearts. For too long in my experience, mechanistic and bureaucratic organisations and indeed professional groups have sought simply to recruit hands, heads and hearts and convert them into nothing more than hands. They have forgotten about heads and hearts. Coaching leaders use the full capability that comes with every pair of hands. They engage the heart and head, enabling team members to build awareness, responsibility and self-belief. These are the building blocks within every individual that leaders can use if they wish to transform healthcare delivery. Such leaders coach; they use questioning to encourage individuals to think, reflect and change because they want to change. This approach makes people feel genuinely involved, committed and more able to learn and adapt. As for the coaching leader he or she may initially fear the loss of control over the pair of hands as those hands begin to make choices and change the way things get done, but in return the leader gets self-reliant and highly effective team members.

To illustrate this point, I have been and am currently working with a variety of NHS organisations but prefer to illustrate the impact of coaching with reference to a simple story a friend told me. This friend is someone who develops coaching skills in NHS organisations. She told me about a vascular surgeon. He described how his juniors were writing discharge letters of epic proportions; he had told them that these letters needed to be shorter so that they could spend more time responding and interacting with patients and their families. This approach had little effect. He then, a couple of weeks later told them again, only this time a little louder. The effect was again short-term. Eventually he, in his own words, 'let them have it with both barrels'. The change to discharge letters was again limited but perhaps more importantly the relationship with the juniors was now fractured; he described them as rebellious. Then the coach began to work with the surgeon. Using questioning they explored the consultant's options. He began to spend time discussing the junior's commitment to shorter discharge letters and the barriers that prevented them being more concise. The results of these interactions were improved team relationships, more time with patients, and team members who were better able to learn. These results might seem small. However, the multiplication of this potential effect across the NHS is clearly significant in releasing potential and capability through such a simple change in approach and behaviour.

Finally I would like to point out the transferability of coaching from team to patient interactions. Research points to the fact that those patients who are encouraged to take responsibility, or at least a joint responsibility, for their own health demonstrate better recovery rates. The questioning and empowering skills used to effectively engage patients are similar to, if not the same as, the tools and techniques used by the coaching leader.

The conclusion I offer is as follows. Developing coaching leaders in the NHS will result in enhanced continuous improvement, improved learning, improved relationships, greater creativity and most important of all, better healthcare delivery for NHS users.

PART FIVE

Research, evidence and recommendations

Involving participants in the design and conduct of trials: the ProtecT study

Jenny Donovan

Introduction

Randomised trials are the design of choice for evaluating the effectiveness of interventions, but many trials recruit slowly or include only a small proportion of eligible participants, potentially threatening validity and wasting resources. Rates of recruitment to trials are difficult to ascertain, but have been reported to be as low as 5–10% of eligible patients for cancer trials. Systematic reviews of the literature have identified a number of barriers to participation for clinicians and patients, but indicated that few evaluative studies have been undertaken to understand or improve trial recruitment.

There can be few issues in healthcare as controversial as population screening for prostate cancer. Debate is conducted in the scientific arena, but the controversy is fuelled by considerable polemic and media pressure. This has led to marked differences in policy between the US (where intensive screening has been introduced in some states) and the UK (where it has not). A number of systematic reviews of the literature have detailed the lack of clear evidence for a benefit from population screening and the possibilities of harm. A key issue is that current screening tests will identify prostate tumours in large numbers of men but it is not yet possible to distinguish between those that will behave aggressively and threaten life and those that will remain innocuous. There are no randomised controlled trials to provide robust evidence about which treatment to recommend, and observational data suggest similar outcomes in relation to mortality for the major treatment options (surgery, radiotherapy and monitoring). Each of these treatments can, however, result in damaging side effects, including impotence and incontinence for the radical interventions, and anxiety and the risk of progression for monitoring.

The aim of the ProtecT (prostate testing for cancer and treatment) feasibility study was to establish whether it was possible to recruit patients to a randomised controlled trial of surgery, radiotherapy and active monitoring for localised prostate cancer. Nested within the study was a randomised trial comparing the effectiveness and cost-effectiveness of urologists and nurses in recruiting patients, and the option of recruitment to all three arms (surgery, radiotherapy and monitoring) or the two radical treatments. Detailed qualitative research was also carried out as part of the trial involving in-depth interviews with trial participants and recruitment staff, and tape-recording of the recruitment appointments. Effectively, we embedded the feasibility phase of this controversial trial within qualitative research, allowing us to investigate recruitment issues from the perspectives of trial participants and recruitment staff, as well as to examine the feasibility of the trial.

Methods

Men aged 50–69 years from primary care centres in three cities were invited to attend a 30-minute prostate check clinic appointment in which they were informed about the study and asked to consent to a prostate-specific antigen (PSA) test. Men with a raised PSA were invited for biopsy and further diagnostic tests. Men with confirmed localised prostate cancer were invited to participate in the randomised trial of recruitment, where they were randomised to a nurse or urologist for an 'information' appointment to discuss recruitment to the treatment trial. In the information appointment, the need for the trial was explained in detail, along with the advantages and disadvantages of each treatment, and the recruiter attempted to randomise the patient to the treatment trial or reach a patient-led preference for treatment. In-depth interviews with trial participants explored interpretation of study information. Audio tape-recordings of recruitment appointments enabled scrutiny of content and presentation of study information by recruiters and interpretation by participants.

Results

Between 1999 and 2001, 8505 men from 18 primary care centres attended prostate check clinics, and 12% had raised PSA levels. In total, 224 cases of prostate cancer were found (165 clinically localised). One hundred and fifty (90% of eligible cases) consented to randomisation between a nurse and urologist. Urologists achieved a higher rate of recruitment to the treatment trial (71% compared with 67% for nurses), but this was not statistically significant (chi-square test 0.60), and a cost-minimisation analysis showed that the urologist arm was more expensive because greater salary costs outweighed their tendency for shorter appointments. The three-arm trial was the most popular option, with 84% opting for this, rather than the two-arm trial ($P < 0.001$).

Initial qualitative findings showed that recruiters had difficulty discussing uncertainty and equipoise and unknowingly used terminology that was misinterpreted by participants. Findings from this qualitative research were implemented: the order of presenting treatments was reversed to ensure equivalence;

misinterpreted terms were identified and avoided; the non-radical arm was redefined and specified; and randomisation and clinical equipoise were presented accurately and acceptably. Scrutiny of later appointments examined the impact of changes to content and presentation of information. Consent to randomisation increased from 40% to 70%.

Conclusion

The full-scale three-arm ProtecT randomised trial of treatments, funded by the NHS Research and Development (R&D) HTA Programme, is now underway in nine centres in the UK. The randomisation rate has fluctuated a little over time and by centre, but overall remains in excess of 70%. The use of qualitative research methods has allowed the views of participants and recruitment staff in the ProtecT study to be elicited, understood and incorporated into the design and conduct of the trial. Changes to study information and presentation determined by the qualitative research have resulted in high levels of randomisation acceptable to patients and clinicians. It may be that embedding randomised trials within qualitative studies may enable the most difficult evaluative questions to be tackled, and could have substantial impact on recruitment to apparently routine and uncontroversial trials.

How the pharmaceutical industry gets patients involved in clinical trials

Carol Aliyar

The primary challenge facing most pharmaceutical companies is to reduce the time it takes to develop new and effective medicines. As an industry we have spent enormous sums re-engineering and streamlining the clinical trial process in an attempt to reduce timelines and bring products to market faster. However, current thinking pinpoints patient recruitment and retention as the most significant challenges facing clinical research in the UK. The failure to recruit enough patients on time accounts for 85–95% of all days lost during clinical trials.[1] Is it any wonder therefore that the industry is determined to address this core issue: patient recruitment.

Before we can begin to examine solutions in detail we have to understand the reasons that lead to poor patient recruitment into trials. There are many, the most common are discussed below.

Complex protocol design

The regulations governing the conduct of clinical trials are many and currently evolving. This is not only to ensure that the results are accurate and reliable, but also to protect the rights of patients taking part. Once the purpose of a trial has been decided, a detailed protocol is drafted. The protocol describes in detail how the trial will be conducted. It will describe:

- entry criteria
- the type of patients to be recruited, to include the nature of the disease under research, age, sex and medical history, etc.
- how many patients will be expected take part and for how long will they be in the trial
- the number and detail of study assessments, e.g. blood tests, ECGs, to be performed.

Protocols are designed to meet the development plan for the compound while complying with regulatory and scientific requirements. They must satisfy the concerns of scientific committees who are somewhat removed from the practicalities of recruiting patients. As a result is it any surprise that when investigators, and more importantly patients, are presented with the prospect of a trial, they do not necessarily like what they find?

One company analysing data from eight studies across various indications found that the most common reason for an eligible patient to refuse to participate in a trial was the time constraint inherent in the protocol.

One approach to improve patient participation in clinical trials is therefore to simplify the protocol. It has been suggested that for such an approach to be successful it would require a change in the way industry develops protocols and may benefit from the involvement of patients at much earlier stages in the development process. How could this be achieved?

One way is to establish a patient advisory group.[2] This group could contribute invaluable, pragmatic input to:

- the design and conduct of the trial
- development of patient-centred outcomes
- provide insight on how to make some trials work
- simplify the patient information sheet
- review the materials to be used to support patient recruitment.

For such an approach to be successful the advisory group would have to be totally independent of the sponsor. The advisory group members would be volunteers, who would not be able to participate in the research programme themselves. Otherwise this may be viewed as yet another ploy to gain access to patient groups interested in participating in trials.

Poor site selection

In order to conduct trials we require the support of either GPs or hospital physicians to perform the research. In the past their selection has often been less than systematic, if not serendipitous. The reason these individuals got involved was either a genuine scientific interest in the research area or the opportunity to generate revenue to fund their own local academic research. However, this type of random selection resulted in 30% of investigator sites failing to recruit a single patient. This was unacceptable, and therefore a more analytical approach to selecting sites was required to support a more predictable approach to recruitment of patients into trials. As an industry we often overlook a clinician's interpersonal skills, intuition and experience which they can deploy as investigators to select participants into trials. Investigators' relationships with their patients are paramount and often directly impact a patient's willingness to contribute to research. An investigator must also be able to determine if this patient will be compliant. Do they really understand the trial? What is the patient's motive for participating in the trial? What could be the impact on their home life?

Box A   What makes a good site?

- A highly motivated investigator
- Past experience in conducting research trials
- High interest in the therapy area under research
- Appropriate resources that can be dedicated to research
- An investigator who is trained and implementing good clinical research practice
- One who is familiar with the local research environment (ethics committees, PCT, and research and development committees)
- Good knowledge of their patients
- A flexible approach to patient visit schedules

Patient pool

The next common reason affecting recruitment is the availability of willing research participants. The percentage of patients who participate in clinical trials varies from one disease area to another but the figure widely quoted is 5%. Therefore a novel and somewhat radical approach aimed at improving public awareness and understanding of clinical research is needed to expand the patient pool. Sources of patient information about trials are improving as we observe posters, radio, television and Internet advertising. Such advertisement is subject to ethical review and approval; however, this approval is now much more commonplace as committees appreciate the importance of improving patient awareness.

The assumptions we have made as to why patients take part in research are many, but some of the common ones are:

- volunteers are altruistic
- research gives the opportunity to improve their condition by taking a new drug that is not yet available
- a trial gives access to particular procedures they cannot obtain from their own GP
- it is an opportunity for a free health screen.

The above may make taking part in research attractive to some. However, it is without question that a lot remains to be done to learn about why our key stakeholders participate in research.

The starting point must be to gain a greater understanding of patient views and attitudes to clinical trials. Over two years ago, eight sponsors from both the NHS and industry who were concerned about the decline in UK patient recruitment into clinical trials came together and developed a study to look specifically at patients' attitudes and beliefs to participating in clinical trials.[3] The soon-to-be reported trial, known as Patients' Attitudes to Clinical Trials (PACT), chose to look at the following:

- measuring the support of patients for clinical trials and their perceptions of the benefits
- determining the willingness of selected patient groups to participate, and examining why
- examining the opinion of patients with some knowledge and experience of clinical trials
- developing a standard questionnaire for future use.

The results of this research are eagerly awaited as they will begin to give an insight to the areas for action with our key stakeholders.

Summary

In summary we should remember that the patient of today is more educated and consumer oriented than ever before. If patient recruitment is no longer to be the weakest link in the chain of research it is vital that all the issues above are addressed. Industry must therefore be proactive in working with patients to help them take responsibility for their own health and healthcare. Only by treating patients as stakeholders can we truly expect them to engage and participate in future trials. The patient must be considered as one of the priorities because without the data from the patient there can be no new submission and consequently no new drugs.

References

1   Prieto K (2003) Meeting the challenges to patient recruitment. *Clinical Research Focus* **14** (3): 16–23.

2   Griffiths A (2003) Direct patient involvement in study planning. *Clinical Research Focus* **14 (8)**: 18–21.

3   Jenkinson C (2003) What patients think of clinical research. *Clinical Research Focus* **14** (4): 61–3.

Consumer involvement in trial design and management

Mark Pitman

The Medical Research Council (MRC) is the largest public sector organisation in the UK for directly funding research relating to human health. For more than 60 years it has led the world in developing the methodology for randomised controlled trials, which are still considered the optimum methodology for assessing the effects of particular interventions on defined outcome measures. The MRC continues to play an active role in this area by: providing funding for clinical trials (mainly studies of clinical effectiveness); developing standards for the conduct of studies; and, through grants to universities and MRC research centres, supporting work on trials methodology.[1]

In 2001 the MRC was approached by the CMO for England and asked if it would assist with the establishment of a clinical trial framework to assess the efficacy of potential therapies for the treatment of human prion diseases.

Human prion disease refers to a group of brain illnesses that are believed to result when a normal human protein, the prion protein, adopts an abnormal structure. This change in form is associated with damage to the brain. The most common example is sporadic Cruetzfeldt-Jakob disease (sCJD) that occurs in approximately one person in 1 000 000 in the population. Other forms exist, the most notable being variant CJD (vCJD, 'human mad cow disease'). Although these diseases have different pathogenesis and time courses they are all characterised by rapid neurodegeneration from the point at which clinical symptoms are expressed. There is currently no treatment and death results within months of clinical diagnosis. Thankfully numbers are relatively small compared with some major UK killers such as strokes and cardiovascular disease (50–60 sCJD cases per year in the UK and currently approximately 17 vCJD cases).[2] Nevertheless, these diseases are characterised by long incubation periods and in the case of vCJD it remains uncertain how many members of the population may be 'carriers' and could succumb to disease at a later date.

Designing a trial for this group of diseases holds many challenges including: the fact that the rapid degenerative nature of these diseases means that there is only a small window of opportunity to collect clinical research data; the poor health of patients limits their ability to get to specialist centres for assessments; while regular monitoring would be beneficial to the research this has to be balanced with the ability of patients to participate; the relatively small number of cases reduces the potential statistical power of any study; the desperate need of relatives may mean that traditional randomisation (treatment versus placebo) may be unpopular because if there is a chance of receiving any treatment relatives are likely to want their loved one to have it; and it is not anticipated that the first therapy is going to be the 'penicillin' for CJD, thus any study is likely to be looking for small beneficial changes in the patient's condition.

For any study in this field to be successful it was acknowledged that it would be necessary to enrol as many of the CJD cases in the UK as possible. It was clear that this could only happen with the full support of the families of CJD cases along with their support networks. The MRC therefore decided to take the unprecedented step of formally involving 'consumers' in the designing and management of the study. The first stage was a workshop to aid understanding of trials and to discuss the design of the study specifically for CJD. It included exercises outlining the pathway to developing a trial and how to make a trial robust. It was attended by families, individuals at risk, carers, patient support group representatives, clinicians and scientists. Members of The MRC Clinical Trials Unit and the MRC Prion Unit produced a draft trial protocol that provided a framework for discussion.

The day highlighted that there was strong support for a trial: one that supported good research and that was sensitive to the needs of very sick patients. The day may be best summarised by the following quotations from attendees:

'A rare occasion – where consumers/families really feel that they have been listened to.'

'Everyone at high level is really thinking about the issues.'

A report summarising the activities and views expressed on the day has been published.[3] These views have been taken into consideration and as a result the draft trial protocol has been significantly modified.

In addition, in an effort to maintain consumer input into the trial, the MRC has invited both the patient support groups (The Human BSE (bovine spongiform encephalopathy) Foundation and The CJD Support Network) to have representation on the trial steering committee (TSC). The MRC has also taken the unprecedented step of inviting a consumer to act as a co-chair to the TSC. In all there are four consumer representatives on the committee.

A TSC is established for every MRC trial to monitor and supervise the progress of the trial towards its interim and overall objectives. With an independent chair and a predominance of independence, membership usually includes the trial co-ordinators, trialists, experts in the field, a lay/consumer representative, a statistician and observers.

Conclusions

Testing the efficacy of potential treatments in new disease areas can provide many complex challenges. Scientists and clinicians have frequently dismissed the involvement of consumers in the development of science because they believe the issues are too technical for them to understand. It has been demonstrated in the first proposed trial for CJD that both the patient and the investigator can benefit from consultation on the design of the trial and share a sense of ownership.

Many trials fail due to poor recruitment; we believe that the involvement of consumers in both the design and management of the first CJD trial make a significant contribution to its success.

Acknowledgements

Thanks to: the MRC Clinical Trials Unit and the MRC Prion Unit for designing and co-ordinating the trial; Crowe Associates for facilitating the workshop; the Department of Health for funding of the trial; the relatives and carers of CJD cases for their open and constructive input; the CJD Support Network and The Human BSE Foundation for enthusiasm and support.

References

1 Clinical Trial Guidelines: www.mrc.ac.uk/index/publications/publications-ethics_and_best_practice/publications-clinical_trials_guidelines.htm

2 DH Monthly CJD Statistics: www.info.doh.gov.uk/doh/intpress.nsf/page/2003-0372?OpenDocument

3 MRC CJD Consumer workshop on clinical trials for CJD – report: www.mrc.ac.uk/pdf-cjd_workshop.pdf

Mix and match? Conjectures on heterogeneous trial populations

H Martyn Evans

Clinical data on the safety and value of a new drug are normally obtained by experimenting on a group of carefully screened patients, who should be as homogeneous a group as it is possible to get, with the intention of eliminating systematic biases and uncontrolled variables. These data are used to define new clinical treatments, which are then administered to the relevant general patient population.

But individual patients commonly vary from the trial population patients, to the extent that they themselves would have been excluded from the trial. It is orthodox that, other things being equal, the clinician may prescribe the new treatment to them if they are not *so* different from the trial population as to make the treatment obviously irrelevant.[1] The doctor decides whether, and how far, it will be safe and useful to prescribe to particular patients; this decision is made on the basis of clinical experience and judgement. Such judgements must concern *either* how closely the patient resembles a presumptively typical trial patient *or* how closely the patient resembles other patients within the clinician's experience whose response to this kind of treatment is known. But this entails that before actually treating a given patient, the relationship between his/her response to the treatment and the response(s) of the trial population cannot be known: every treatment episode is an experiment in which the sample size $n = 1$.

Could we do things any differently?

Imagine instead that trial data are obtained by experimenting on a group of patients who are as varied a group as one is likely to encounter in the relevant general patient population (those suffering from the condition at issue). Individual patients *ex hypothesi* now fully match the relevant trial population: they suffer from that condition (above, say, a threshold that distinguishes the condition from normal health). Imagine now simply that the doctor decides whether to prescribe the treatment on the basis of whether or not the patients in the trial were sufficiently helped by it, in the process making a judgement about how likely it was that patients *just like this one* were represented in the trial population. The treatment is still, of course, administered in an experiment in which the sample size, as before, is $n = 1$.

However, this sample size can be increased, and its predictive value strengthened, if we imagine the doctor accessing very detailed information about the relevant personal characteristics of individual trial subjects and their treatment responses. This could readily yield what is effectively a loosely controlled experiment where $n = 2$ – i.e. the index patient plus their nearest 'representative' in the trial. The size of n rises if there are further relevantly similar patients. For patients ineligible for the conventional trial, there is a substantial chance that someone very like them does appear in the alternative trial I am proposing; remember that in a conventional trial there was no chance, for they would have failed the exclusion criteria.

Of course there are powerful reasons to specify a homogeneous trial population. For instance it protects the entry and exit points of the trial, with specific levels of disease standardised upon entry, enabling us to specify (and, hopefully, to attribute to the experimental treatment) the difference that has occurred during the trial period. But notice that this can be achieved with a heterogeneous trial population as well, if we focus closely on each individual's clinical progress (derived from their individual entry and exit points) and try to express this in numerical terms that would allow comparability with the results from other patients. (Although difficult, conceptually, this is child's play in the context of what is attempted in the derivation of QALYs.) Of course some other features of homogenous trial populations could not be mimicked in a heterogeneous population, specifically the ability to control for extraneous variables and to eliminate sources of systematic bias. The data from a heterogeneous patient population would be so contaminated as to be scarcely usable in the orthodox view.

The outrageous question I wish to ask is: Does this matter? Well, yes: but my sceptical suggestion is that it may matter less than we think.

First, all data become contaminated in practice. The purity of data from conventional homogeneous trial populations is itself compromised when we prescribe the trialled treatment to any patients who would have been ineligible for the trial (e.g. if their levels of disease are significantly different from that demanded by the trial then the validity and applicability of the trial's entry point are compromised).

Second, clinical practice is mysterious. Since all clinical interactions are inherently individual, they themselves logically cannot be made the subject of population-level evidence gathering of the type constituted within clinical trials. It is hard to see how an evidence-based medicine (EBM)-type study of what happens at the individual level could be coherent. If clinical practice works, EBM itself cannot show that it does.

So, third, it follows that the strict chain of actions, involving clinical appeal to data derived at a population level, ends either in inaction or in something undemonstrable within EBM (personal communication, Professor APS Hungin). It may end in inaction because, since no treatment is logically capable of crossing the gap between a carefully screened population and an unsanitised collection of varying individuals, one concludes that one must stay one's hand. Orthodox population-level data tell us about the probabilities of a treatment response attaching to different subgroups in the trial population (the groups are defined in relation to their response). The trouble is that we don't know which is the relevant subgroup – the 'reference class' – for any subsequent patient until after treating them. Or alternatively the chain of actions ends in something undemonstrable from the EBM standpoint: actions which necessarily stray beyond what would be sanctioned by the strict application of population-level data constitute a leap of faith, sanctioned psychologically rather than logically.

Finally, the difference between the experimental setting of a controlled trial and the naturalistic setting of clinical practice is qualitative, not quantitative. The coherence of generalised evidence from a conventional population-level study is discarded when we apply such results to the individual patient. Unlike the objects of physics or chemistry, medicine's objects – people – cannot ultimately be abstracted from their naturalistic context, in which their behaviour and responses are necessarily individualised.

We can know a great deal about the probabilities concerning what happens to specified proportions of them in closely defined, non-naturalistic circumstances. But the question is whether this is of any help now in treating the Mrs Jones in front of us. To find *this* out, we have to treat her, wait, and see. My suggestion is that this significantly constrains the advantages of using a homogeneous trial population, leaving the heterogeneous trial population looking unexpectedly attractive.

Reference

1   Sackett DL, Straus SE, Richardson WS, Rosenberg W and Haynes RB (2000) *Evidence-based Medicine: how to practice and teach EBM*. Churchill Livingstone: Edinburgh, pp. 118–19.

The Interventional Procedures Programme

Bruce Campbell and Tom Dent

The Interventional Procedures Programme has come of age this year, publishing the first national guidance of its kind in brief, pragmatic format. Each guidance document comprises general recommendations, followed by background information about the procedure, and then specific sections on efficacy and safety, which include published data and the opinions of specialist advisors. Some guidance concludes with miscellaneous comments of the Advisory Committee, such as uncertainty about long-term outcomes. Any recommendations about training or submission of data to registries are specific, and are made with reference to the relevant professional organisations.

The initial task of the Interventional Procedures Advisory Committee (IPAC) was to consider the list of procedures which SERNIP (the Safety and Efficacy Register for New Interventional Procedures – now no longer in existence) had classified other than as safe and efficacious – some no longer very 'new'. These have been discussed and the programme has settled into its longer-term mode of receiving notification of new procedures through its website. About six of these notifications come each month from a variety of sources, including doctors, professional organisations, industry and the public.

There will always be some uncertainty about exactly what constitutes a new procedure: how much does an existing procedure need to be modified to be 'new'? However, there should be no doubt that the programme is committed to reviewing the safety and efficacy of *procedures* and not of devices. As a rule, any fully trained clinician planning to undertake a procedure for the first time should consult the NICE website to check on its status.

When a new procedure is notified to NICE, the interventional procedures team makes initial enquiries to see whether it merits consideration by the committee. Thereafter, two things happen. First the team prepares an 'overview', which includes background information and the results of a litera-ture search. The amount and quality of published information varies greatly and is sometimes very sparse. When more exists, the most valid studies are selected for presentation to IPAC. The importance of producing timely guidance militates against a full systematic review of every procedure, and the aim is to present the most significant data which will guide a decision about safety and efficacy. If ever important published data are missed in the overview, then the public consultation period offers a valuable opportunity for interested parties to point this out: notification of unincluded yet potentially important data is always welcomed and followed up.

The second action after notification of a procedure is to identify and consult specialist advisors. This is done through professional organisations whose medical members may undertake the procedure; there may be more than one of these. The aspiration is to secure advice from nationally recognised specialists who are carrying out the procedure, and also from knowledgeable specialists who are not. They will not always include those individuals conducting the largest numbers of a procedure, unless such people are nominated by their national body. This approach aims to select advisors who are held in high regard by their colleagues; they will not necessarily be enthusiasts, with the bias which can accompany such enthusiasm. The specialist advisors are asked a series of questions about the current and likely future use of the procedure, its efficacy and possible concerns about safety.

IPAC considers the overview and advisors' opinions. Their draft guidance may then recommend that the evidence on safety and efficacy seems adequate; or that uncertainty exists; or occasionally a procedure may be deemed unsafe or inefficacious. If the evidence is not considered adequate, this does not mean that the procedure should not be used, but that it should be used judiciously, and that publication of more data will be valuable. Specifically, and most importantly, clinicians wishing to use the procedure should ensure that patients offered it understand the uncertainty. NICE produces information for patients about each procedure, to supplement the clinician's own explanation. NICE has also agreed with the Department of Health a form of words which may be used to support written consent in such cases.

Clinicians wishing to undertake a procedure with uncertain safety and efficacy are required by the guidance to audit outcomes thoroughly. Before they embark on the procedure, however, they should inform the clinical governance lead of their trust. The response of trusts to such approaches is important to the maintenance of innovation in the NHS. There is no intention that NICE guidance should be used as a reason to prevent properly trained and equipped clinicians from embarking on new procedures, provided they meet the conditions that the guidance specifies. Indeed, if they intend to collect their outcome data for publication or submission to a registry then there is advantage in their efforts, because this will reduce uncertainty about the procedure's safety and efficacy. The guidance will sometimes specify a registry for national data submission and it may highlight particular uncertainties which audit or research should address (for example quality of life measures or long-term outcomes).

Whatever form IPAC's preliminary recommendations take, they are subject to public consultation via NICE's website for a month. All those who have expressed an interest in the procedure, specialist groups, patient groups (identified by NICE's Patient Involvement Unit) and interested device manufacturers are alerted to the consultation period. All consultation responses are considered by IPAC. Any factual errors or important missing evidence mentioned by consultees are pursued. We particularly welcome focused consultation responses which suggest changes and which are accompanied by supporting evidence or reasoning. Consultees also need to understand that the guidance must be brief to be useful.

The guidance is amended in the light of consultation responses and is then considered by the NICE Guidance Executive before being published in English and Welsh, accompanied by information for the public. Hard copies are circulated to all relevant specialists and to trusts, and the guidance is available on the NICE website.

Most interventional procedures guidance is not scheduled for review, but if there is uncertainty and if potentially important publications are expected then a review date may be set. Alternatively, there is always the opportunity for interested parties to refer a procedure back to the programme if they believe that new information makes that appropriate. The programme's outputs are intended to be timely and responsive to clinicians, patients and others affected by the use of procedures.

To succeed, the Interventional Procedures Programme must balance the acquisition and analysis of adequate information against the publication of guidance without undue delay. This depends on close collaboration with all those involved in the use of procedures, who set its agenda and who take the time to offer helpful comment and opinion.

What is the role of research and evidence in policy making?

Martin Eccles

Introduction

NICE has a series of programmes, including technology appraisals and clinical guidelines, which deal daily with the realities of incorporating evidence into policy.[1] If we regard NICE as only one specific example, are there common issues that will confront researchers and policy makers as they attempt to interact in an effort to integrate evidence into policy making? In this article I use the term policy maker in a general way, denoting anyone who is responsible for making allocation decisions about the provision of healthcare; they may do this at any point within the healthcare system from a local to a national level.

The concept that published research should influence policy is, on the one hand, a self-evidently desirable aim and on the other an invitation to step into a world of politics and misunderstandings. Misunderstanding is exemplified by the suggestion of Caplan *et al* that policy makers and researchers inhabit two different (and separate) worlds in one of which researchers see themselves as rational, objective and open to new ideas while seeing policy makers as action and interest-oriented and indifferent to evidence and new ideas.[2] In the other world policy makers see themselves as responsible, action oriented and pragmatic, and researchers as naïve, jargon ridden and irresponsible in relationship to practical realities.[2] That this is political territory is illustrated by Fox and Oxman who suggest that there are three different sets of politics at play – the politics of research, the politics of health policy and the politics of collaboration between researchers and policy makers.[3]

While there is a published literature suggesting how to integrate research findings into policy, this is largely opinion-based with little empirical data describing the effectiveness of strategies to achieve this. In this article I have drawn on three pieces of empirical research to illustrate some of the generalities that need to be considered when contemplating the relationship between evidence and policy making. This is not a systematic review of the literature and thus will inevitably be partial and incomplete; however, I hope that it is informative and will act as a signpost into this area for readers.

Accountability and evidence

Researcher's accountability is to their research community (including research funders) and to those policy makers they would aspire to have use their results. They are accountable for the validity of their methods and the truth of their studies.

For policy makers the position is different. Their accountability is to the public and is for the decisions that they take. However, in taking their decisions they will take into account a range of factors of which scientific research is only one. They will also take account of other factors such as financial implications, public opinion, political climate, the actions of interest groups and the views of opinion leaders. Sometimes they will take more account of these other factors than they will of research evidence. What do we know of the factors that influence them in taking their decisions?

Barriers and facilitators to the use of evidence in policy making

Innvaer and colleagues systematically reviewed the literature on health policy makers' perceptions of factors promoting or inhibiting their use of evidence.[4] From 24 studies reporting a total of 2041 interviews they identified commonly reported facilitators and barriers. The three most commonly reported facilitators were personal contact (13/24 studies), timely relevance (13/24) and the inclusion of summaries with recommendations (11/24), while the four most commonly reported barriers were absence of personal contact (11/24), lack of timeliness or relevance of research (9/24), mutual mistrust (8/24), and power and budget struggles (7/24).

Others have approached these issues in a different way. *Informing Judgment: case studies of health policy and research in six countries* is a description of six case studies of the inter-relationship between policy and research evidence.[3] The case studies demonstrate the importance of context yet also draw generalisable lessons across the differing countries, with their range of histories, cultures and decisions. In their introduction to the report, Fox and Oxman suggest there are a number of generalisations that can be made from the case studies (*see* Box A) over and above the single statement that 'The proper purpose of collaboration between researchers and policy makers is to use evidence from research to inform judgments for which policy makers are accountable.'

In a further case report, Scheel *et al.* described a study where a further dimension of the relationship between researchers, evidence and policy makers was illustrated – the non-use of research findings.[5] The authors describe a collaboration between researchers and policy makers designing and running a randomised controlled trial to evaluate two strategies to implement a return to work policy (Active Sick Leave – ASL). However, the collaboration appeared to

---

Box A Generalisations on the relationship between researchers, evidence and policy makers (Adapted from Fox and Oxman, 2001)[3]

- Because both research and policy making are complex activities and very different from each other, mutual understanding requires conscious effort. To inform policy making more effectively, researchers need better systematic understanding of political culture.
- Policy makers can help achieve mutual understanding by respecting researchers' knowledge, competence and needs.
- Policy makers and researchers must learn to accommodate differences in the time frames within which they operate.
- Collaboration builds on good experiences for both researchers and policy makers. To achieve good experiences, a policy maker said, the 'rules of engagement must include appropriate expectations and appropriate definitions of success'.
- Effective collaboration between researchers and policy makers is likely to be enhanced if both groups continue to work together after the policy-making process to evaluate the results of implementing the policy.
- Trust between individuals is built up over years. The process of making health policy should create and maintain opportunities for long-term collaboration between policy makers and researchers when this is possible.

---

fracture when the policy makers did not wait for the final results of the trial. During the course of the trial it became apparent that there was an external policy move to use ASL more generally, in the expectation that it would reduce time off work by 20%. The strategy to be used in this policy was one that the trial had already demonstrated did not increase the uptake of ASL. In addition, when the final results of the trial became available, showing no effect of either strategy to implement ASL on time off work, disability or quality of life, they were ignored by most of the policy makers involved.

This example of non-use raises the question of what is expected from the 'use' of research findings. In their review of health policy makers' perceptions of factors promoting or inhibiting their use of evidence, Innvaer and colleagues describe three types of use – direct, selective and enlightening.[4] These three can be regarded as points on a continuum from a piece of research fully and totally answering a policy need, through to a piece of research stimulation thinking or insight around a policy decision but having no direct impact. The ASL example, at most an example of enlightening, more realistically suggests the need for a fourth category of explicit non-use of research findings as it seems to represent a circumstance where factors other than research evidence outweigh any impact of the research evidence so much that it is not used.

Some realities

Having identified the importance of mutual understanding, effective communication and mutual trust it is then appropriate to consider something of the realities of researchers and policy makers trying to interact. Lomas described a number of challenges, for both researchers and policy makers, identified by Canada's Health Services Research Foundation bringing together a group of researchers and policy makers and asking them to describe the realities of trying to interact with each other.[6] The group identified the differing time lines of the two constituencies and added a lack of available time for both groups. They also identified that, in most systems, there are multiple researchers and multiple policy makers with no clear points of contact between, or entry points into, their respective worlds. From outside there is often no way of knowing who within a system is influential and who is not; added to this is the fact that neither population is stable, both being prey to personnel changes and restructuring. Finally, they suggested that there is only limited mutual understanding of technical issues; researchers don't understand the technical aspects of policy making and policy makers don't understand the technicalities of research method.

Conclusions

It is tempting to suggest that the solution is to address the generalisations that Fox and Oxman describe.[3] However, Lomas's realities reflect the *real politic* of researchers and policy makers interacting and emphasise the view of all the authors cited in this article – there are no simple solutions.[6] As Fox and Oxman suggest, 'both policy makers and researchers must continue struggling to help ensure that judgements about health policies are well informed by research evidence. The alternative is to acquiesce to poorly informed health policies'.[3]

Acknowledgements

I am grateful to Andy Oxman and Jeremy Grimshaw for their advice.

References

1   Dillon A, Gibbs TG, Riley T and Sheldon TA (2001) The National Institute for Clinical Excellence and coverage of Relenza by the NHS. In: D Fox and A Oxman (eds) *Informing Judgment: case studies of health policy and research in six countries*. Milbank Memorial Fund: New York.

2   Caplan N, Morrison A and Stambaugh RJ (1975) *The Use of Social Science Knowledge in Policy Decisions at the National Level: a report to respondents*. The University of Michigan: Ann Harbor, Michigan, pp. 1–63.

3 Fox D and Oxman A (eds) (2001) *Informing Judgment: case studies of health policy and research in six countries.* Milbank Memorial Fund: New York.

4 Innvaer S, Vist G, Trommald M and Oxman AD (2002) Health policy-makers' perceptions of their use of evidence: a systematic review. *Journal of Health Services Research and Policy* **7**: 239–44.

5 Scheel IB, Hagen KB and Oxman AD (2003) The unbearable lightness of healthcare policy making: a description of a process aimed at giving it some weight. *Journal of Epidemiology and Community Health* **57**: 1–5.

6 Lomas J (2000) Using 'Linkage and Exchange' to move research into policy at a Canadian foundation. *Health Affairs* **19**: 236–40.

What is the role of research and evidence in cancer policy?

Robert Haward

Introduction

This article uses cancer care to illustrate the influence of evidence on policy development. The first comprehensive cancer policy in the UK was developed by the Chief Medical Officers (CMOs) of England and Wales and known as Calman–Hine, published in 1995.[1] This was the first time a major disease had been covered by a single policy, and paved the way for the national strategic frameworks for other disease groups such as coronary heart disease.

The development of the policy followed mounting disquiet about the adequacy and performance of UK health services for cancer patients. There was striking consistency in the issues coming forward from patient groups, cancer professionals and in media coverage. These were reinforced in published studies.[2–5] The main concern was the variability in management experienced by patients. This was exacerbated by the 'lottery' of referral, whether patients had early access to cancer specialists (surgeons and oncologists) or only to generalists. Experience suggested this process operated erratically, yet influenced the subsequent management and outcomes for many people.

Cancer policy: the Calman–Hine initiative

The two CMOs secured a political mandate to develop cancer policy, a field in which both had considerable personal knowledge. The mechanism they used to develop their policy was unusual in that they established a small expert advisory group to prepare the policy document and gave them an unusually 'free hand' in so doing. This group elected to meet experts and consider research evidence on several important themes, namely:

- international comparisons:
  - of outcomes
  - of inputs to cancer care (manpower, facilities and resources)
- the performance of cancer services in the UK

- alternative models for delivering cancer services
- the importance of specialisation and caseload.

The evidence was not presented in the policy document itself, but Selby and colleagues published a summary on behalf of the group.[5] The evidence base for moving from a generic to a specialist multidisciplinary model was particularly crucial and some UK studies were particularly influential, notably the ones by Gillis, Junor and Sainsbury.[6–8] Although the policy was subject to consultation, its content and format were largely unchallenged. The policy received a broadly supportive reception from patient and professional audiences.

Calman–Hine has been hugely influential as a framework of principles, structures and processes for good cancer care. It did not cover specific issues for each type of cancer, such as personnel, facilities, clinical organisation, and the effectiveness of diagnostic and treatment modalities.

Service guidance: the 'Improving Outcomes' project

Immediately following the publication of Calman–Hine the Department of Health established a programme to produce guidance for each site of cancer. Service guidance was aimed at those responsible for commissioning or managing the delivery of cancer services, including cancer networks. It specified the clinical structures and processes necessary for each site of cancer (or group of sites, e.g. gynaecological malignancies) if good outcomes were to be achieved. Published policy has so far covered breast, colorectal and lung cancers together with gynaecological, upper gastrointestinal, urological and haematological malignancies; these represent about 80% of cancers in the UK (based on incidence, excluding non-melanoma skin cancer). Further titles are planned.

The development methodology was derived from an intensive exercise at the outset, and has remained largely unchanged. It utilises evidence of all kinds, including clinical effectiveness but falls short of the level of clinical detail appropriate for practice guidelines. The published format evolved during work on the first topic (breast cancer). The methodology and role of the project has been described by Haward.[9,10] Each manual is accompanied by a comprehensive tabulated summary of the evidence prepared by the Centre for Reviews and Dissemination at York University which co-ordinates the evidence reviews.

Service guidance: using evidence

A wide range of evidence is used to formulate service guidance. Health service information, audit data, cancer registry and epidemiological studies are used to examine variations in the performance and outcome of current services, and to make comparisons with other health systems. This gives important indications about the need for change, although expert advice is often required to interpret such material.

The strongest evidence is derived from systematic reviews where these are available, more usually individual trials and observational studies need to be assessed. Many important questions about services have never been tested in well-designed studies, and expert opinion may be the only guide in formulating some recommendations. Service guidance cannot ignore crucial issues in the care pathway, such as referral criteria, follow-up arrangements, or palliative support, merely because no high-quality peer-reviewed papers exist. The key to deploying such varied evidence is transparency and clarity to ensure that users can examine the evidence base supporting particular recommendations.

Service guidance: factors influencing service organisation

Figure A illustrates the concept that the optimum arrangement of services is influenced by several components which may overlap. For example volume and specialisation go together, making it difficult to establish the relationships between individual factors and outcomes. This literature has grown in recent years with several systematic reviews.[11–15]

In a forceful editorial Hillner described the cumulative weight of this evidence; 123 of 128 published studies showed a volume–quality relationship.[12] In oncology he identified consistent and often striking examples of better outcomes with higher volume. Hillner argued that this evidence should be

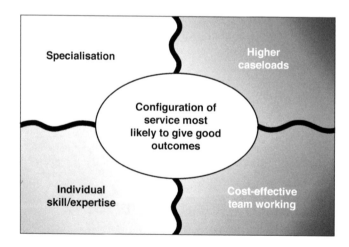

Figure A Schematic representation of factors influencing service configuration.

considered more seriously as a driver for change in cancer care, concluding that 'if these decisions did not involve livelihood, prestige, and power, we would have demanded action long ago'.[12]

This evidence has been taken seriously in the preparation of cancer service guidance, despite the difficulties in interpretation of the evidence. There are possibilities for bias, including case-mix adjustment, publication bias and the statistical limitations of examining single dimensions of multifaceted issues. The guidance developers have made recommendations for those cancers for which there is sound evidence of benefit, setting appropriate thresholds for the UK context.

Conclusions

In the last decade cancer policy making has been innovative and productive. Throughout this process evidence has been utilised more extensively and systematically than ever before, although limited by weaknesses and gaps in available evidence.

These policies are changing the delivery of cancer services, with improved clinical decisions and patient management. These changes will lead to better outcomes. Key changes include:

- more resources: particularly manpower and facilities, with well-defined structures, service inter-relationships and clinical processes
- multidisciplinary teams: site specialists making clinical decisions together about managing their patients
- reduced fragmentation of care: all patients are referred to identified site specialists working in multidisciplinary teams, each with a clear remit and sufficient caseload
- reconfiguration: high morbidity and mortality procedures are managed in hospitals with extensive experience and expertise.

References

1   Department of Health (1995) *Policy Framework for Commissioning Cancer Services: a report by the Expert Advisory Group on Cancer to the Chief Medical Officers of England and Wales.* HM Stationery Office: London.

2   Chouillet AM, Bell CMJ and Hiscox JG (1994) Management of breast cancer in southeast England. *British Medical Journal* **308**: 168–71.

3   Richards MA, Wolfe CD, Tilling K, Barton J, Bourne HM and Gregory WM (1996) Variations in the management and survival of women under 50 years with breast cancer in the South East Thames region. *British Journal of Cancer* **73**: 751–7.

4   Sainsbury R, Rider L, Smith A, Macadam A and The Yorkshire Breast Cancer Group

(1995) Does it matter where you live? Treatment variation for breast cancer in Yorkshire. *British Journal of Cancer* **71**: 1275–8.

5 Selby P, Gillis C and Haward R (1996) Benefits from specialised cancer care. *Lancet* **348**: 313–18.

6 Gillis CR and Hole DJ (1996) Survival outcome of care by specialist surgeons in breast cancer: a study of 3786 patients in the west of Scotland. *British Medical Journal* **312**: 145–8.

7 Junor EJ, Hole DJ and Gillis CR (1994) Management of ovarian cancer: referral to a multidisciplinary team matters. *British Journal of Cancer* **70**: 363–70.

8 Sainsbury R, Haward B, Rider L, Johnston C and Round C (1995) Influence of clinician workload and patterns of treatment on survival from breast cancer. *Lancet* **345**: 1265–70.

9 Haward RA (2003) Making and monitoring cancer policy in the United Kingdom: the cancer registry contribution. In: R Sankila, R Black, J Coebergh *et al.* (eds) *Evaluation of Clinical Care by Cancer Registries*. IARC Technical Publication No. 37, pp. 39–46.

10 Haward RA (2003) Using service guidance to shape the delivery of cancer services: experience in the UK. *British Journal of Cancer* **89 (Suppl 1)**: S12–14.

11 Halm EA, Lee C and Chassin MR (2002) Is volume related to outcome in health care? A systematic review and methodological critique of the literature. *Annals of Internal Medicine* **137**: 511–20.

12 Hillner BE, Smith TJ and Desch CE (2000) Hospital and physician volume or specialisation and outcomes in cancer treatment: importance in quality of cancer care. *Journal of Clinical Oncology* **18**: 2327–40.

13 Hewitt M and Petitti D (eds) (2001) *Interpreting the Volume: outcome relationship in the context of cancer care*. National Academies Press: Washington DC.

14 Teisberg P, Hansen FH, Hotvedt R *et al.* (2001) *SMM Report 2/2001: Hospital Volume and Quality of Health Outcome*. The Norwegian Centre for Health: Oslo.

15 Smith TS, Hillner B and Bear HD (2003) Taking action on the volume–quality relationship: how long can we hide our heads in the colostomy bag? *Journal of the National Cancer Institute* **95 (10)**: 695–7.

The role of evidence in improving market access

Julia Earnshaw

Introduction

Since the 1960s and the introduction of regulation on the use of medicines, prescribing has become increasingly evidence based. As well as the assessment of efficacy, safety and quality prior to gaining a product licence, any commercial claims made by manufacturers concerning the benefits of medicines have been regulated by the Association of The British Pharmaceutical Industry (ABPI) Code of Practice.[1] Despite this evidence-based approach, individual prescribing decisions were still influenced by factors such as personal experience, values and beliefs, and influence from others. As a result considerable variation in prescribing remained and a number of initiatives have been introduced to address this. These included the widespread establishment of local drug and therapeutics committees, the promotion of practice formularies and clinical guidelines and employment of local prescribing advisors. Many of these initiatives drew on evidence to inform their recommendations; however, variable decision making continued, leading to 'postcode prescribing'. In 1998 the publication of *A First Class Service* proposed the initiation of the NICE to make evidence-based recommendations on the appropriate use of medicines at a national level.[2] These local and national initiatives effectively formed an additional 'fourth hurdle' before medicines could be used in the NHS. The term 'market access' has been coined to reflect the need by manufacturers to overcome this hurdle.

How does evidence inform market access decisions?

The emergence of new decision makers on the use of medicines has resulted in the need for additional evidence. In addition to the traditional information on efficacy, quality and safety, the manufacturers increasingly have to provide additional evidence, including clinical and cost-effectiveness. To meet these needs GlaxoSmithKline provide a range of information at different stages of the medicines life cycle.

During development, information is provided on a six-monthly basis to those in the NHS responsible for planning budgets at a local and national level. A document provides background information on products in development with more detailed information on compounds likely to have budgetary impact in the next three years. More detailed information is provided in Advanced Planning Information/Formulary Packs in the six months prior to launch to inform local decision making and planning.

How is evidence used in decision making by NICE?

Evidence also plays a key role in defining topics that will be selected for review by NICE. Information provided to the Horizon Scanning Centre identifies potential subjects for NICE appraisal. Specific feedback on consultation documents ensures that the evidence available to inform the topic selection process is accurate and up to date.

Once a topic has been selected for review by NICE it enters the appraisal process. The recent draft *Guide to the Methods of Technology Appraisal* stated 'consideration of an inclusive and high-quality evidence base is fundamental to the appraisal process'.[3] The evidence base includes an independent assessment from one of the HTA groups, and submissions from manufacturers and sponsors, patient and carer groups, healthcare professionals and clinical specialists/patient experts. In a typical submission to NICE, GlaxoSmithKline would provide:

- details and results of all relevant (within licence) clinical trials for which we are the sponsor or that are known to us
- listings of other clinical trials that are not relevant, e.g. outside scope
- if appropriate, a systematic review and meta-analysis of studies
- other research evidence where relevant to the scope, e.g. cohort/observational studies/epidemiology/burden of illness
- cost-effectiveness evidence including an electronic copy of any model used
- NHS budget impact information.

However, there is a recognition that despite this evidence-based approach it is unlikely that perfect information will exist. This is particularly the case for new medicines where the regulatory clinical trials may well provide imperfect evidence due to factors such as choice of comparator, length of follow up, use of intermediate endpoints and lack of generalisability. Hence decisions will still be taken under conditions of uncertainty. The need for other factors to be taken into account is also recognised in the draft *Guide to the Methods of Technology Appraisal*.[3] This document flags the difference between the two stages in the NICE process, those of assessment and appraisal. Appraisal is defined as:

'A consideration of the outputs of the assessment process within the context of additional information … The appraisal committee translates the evidence available in the assessment report and elsewhere into an appraisal decision, applying judgements on the importance of a range of factors that may vary from appraisal to appraisal.'

The impact of these judgements is clear when the range of cost-effectiveness values in medicines approved by NICE is considered (*see* Figure A).[4]

To what extent do NICE decisions inform local decision making and improve market access?

It is now mandatory for local decision makers to fund medicines that have received a recommendation by NICE. In theory therefore, except for demographic variation, one would expect similar use of NICE-recommended medicines. In reality there remains significant variability – for example recent data suggests that the uptake of trastuzurnab (Herceptin) remains variable, with many patients not receiving this treatment despite a positive NICE recommendation.[5] So why is this?

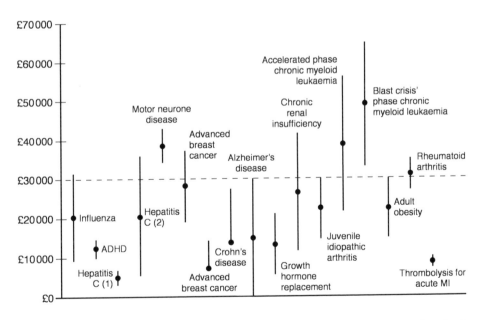

Figure A Range of cost/quality adjusted life years values in technologies approved by NICE. ADHD: attention deficit hyperactivity disorder; MI: myocardial infarction.

The Management of Medicines (MANMED) survey in 2001 assessed primary care organisations' (PCOs') and hospital trusts' approach to medicines management.[6] Specifically they asked what action had been taken in response to the NICE guidance on proton pump inhibitors and rosiglitazone. The level of response ranged from no action to nine types of action. The same project also reviewed the literature on the success of alternative approaches to medicines management and found that although a wide range of approaches is possible, there is little evidence of what is most effective. Subsequently GlaxoSmithKline has undertaken market research with 50 prescribing advisors across the UK; 64% agreed that their PCO prioritised implementation of some areas of NICE guidance over others. A range of factors impacted on which guidance was most likely to be prioritised, including whether the guidance was linked to a national target, whether it was an issue locally and whether it supported current clinical practice. Clearly therefore values and judgements made at a local level will impact on the implementation of NICE guidance. As a result, despite the introduction of NICE, market access barriers will still exist at a local level affecting the use of specific medicines.

Conclusions

A range of mechanisms has been introduced that provide additional hurdles beyond the regulatory process and restrict the uptake of medicines within the NHS. Despite the evidence-based nature of these hurdles, value judgements and other factors continue to influence decisions and their implementation. Therefore although evidence is clearly critical to achieving market access, it is unlikely that this will be the only factor in the uptake of new medicines.

References

1   *Code of Practice for the Pharmaceutical Industry 2003*. The Association of the British Pharmaceutical Industry: London.

2   Department of Health (1998) *A First Class Service: quality in the new NHS*. Department of Health: London.

3   National Institute for Clinical Excellence (2003) *Guide to the Methods of Technology Appraisal*. Draft for consultation, August 2003. NICE: London.

4   www.nice.org.uk

5   Editorial (2003) NICE guidance on Herceptin not being implemented. *Scrip* **2895**: 6.

6   Mason A, Towse A, Drummond M and Cooke J (2002) *Influencing Prescribing in a Primary Care Led NHS*. Office of Health Economics: London.

The role of health economics in making recommendations to the NHS

Martin Buxton

Introduction

In an independent review by WHO, the appraisal function of NICE was hailed as an important model for technology appraisals internationally.[1] The commitment to rigorous methodology was applauded. It is clear to all that the analysis of cost-effectiveness (CEA) is central to this methodology, and revised guidance on the Institute's preferences for the presentation of CEA is shortly to be issued.[2] However, there is a continuing debate as to whether NICE guidance is always implemented as fully or as quickly as it might be, despite the obligation on the NHS to do so.[3,4] The impression is that implementation is patchy.

This may be a manifestation of resistance to more central control over local spending priorities. However, it may also reflect a disconnection between the analyses that underlie NICE's consideration of cost-effectiveness and the short-term managerial and political reality of the NHS. The WHO review team suggested that NICE needs to address more fully the local budgetary implications of adopting technologies that have been appraised on the basis of their acceptable cost-effectiveness ratio.[1]

The problems behind the rationality of cost-effectiveness analyses

CEAs for NICE are very appropriately required to take account of all NHS and personal social service costs. For example, analysis may suggest that the additional costs of the GP prescribing of a new drug would lead to a subsequent reduction in the patients' use of specialist tertiary services. These might have earmarked funding from the National Specialist Commissioning Advisory Group. In such a case, the reasonable net cost to the NHS on which NICE focuses, might hide widespread increases in primary care prescribing budgets counterbalanced by savings focused in a quite different NHS budget. What is more, the costs and savings are rarely contemporaneous. Typically in health, we invest up front to achieve future health benefits and so the cost savings (that future improved health may bring) may occur a long way ahead. Many of the interventions that NICE has recommended may have benefits (and associated cost savings) that are not fully realised for 20 years or more.

CEA handles this in part by allowing for the fact that society has preferences for benefits sooner rather than later and the costs later rather than sooner. But the strength of this preference, which is exhibited in the chosen discount rate(s), is set by HM Treasury. They now judge that the appropriate rate of discount is 3.5% per annum for costs and benefits.[5]

The assumption is that society can achieve costless transfers between budgets and at the discount rate in question, between time periods. That is not the managerial reality in the NHS. Budgets are not easily adjusted. Nor are managers generally able to transfer funds intertemporally. I suspect that the PCT finance officer who argues that his current serious overspending will be easily met from a reduction in someone else's budgets 20 years hence would be forfeiting his performance-related pay!

Furthermore, these CEA studies typically take no account of transition costs, but reflect the situation in a new steady state.

So the assumptions within CEA do not accord with the managerial reality, or necessarily with the political priorities manifest in other pressures on the health service.

Possible solutions

So what can be done? Some might suggest that NICE could place less attention on CEA and more on budget impact in making its decisions. That would be a retrograde step. However, a simple and positive step would be to provide a much more detailed and disaggregated budget impact statement. This should not be difficult to achieve if the underlying cost-effectiveness studies are well constructed. Suitably presented, this would enable all parties at a local level to see and understand the balance of costs between different parts of the NHS and how it changes over time.

Disaggregated costs from each set of guidance could then be netted up to see what is implied for aggregate shifts in budgets over time. It may be that, by fortunate chance, the net effects balance out, or the shift in pressure on particular budgets is marginal. If so, the detailed evidence to show that will prove to be a reassurance. If they do not balance out, then budget allocations for the following years could be adjusted to reflect any significant imbalances.

Moreover, if at some point there were to be earmarking of funds for NICE advances, then this annual totting up of where costs are falling would help ensure that the funds were appropriately allocated at the 'micro-level'.

Discussion and conclusion

The current and proposed methodological guidance does not reflect a pure welfare-economics perspective. If, as many economists would argue it should, NICE were concerned about, and gave equal weight to, costs and cost savings, including those falling on parties other than the NHS and personal social services, the problem would be very much greater. Even within the NHS, costs may fall disproportionately on certain budgets. The recent focus on new cancer drugs may itself have meant that certain budgets were disproportionately stretched. Where problems are foreseen at a micro-level, there should be clearer and more specific expectations from NICE as to how soon, and how fast, a technology should be introduced, so facilitating local micro-planning.

NICE should not back away from the rational process of basing its decisions about the introduction of new (or occasionally the withdrawal of existing) technologies on the balance between the health benefits they provide and the net costs they impose to the health system as a whole. But all parties must recognise that this rational economic logic does not necessarily fit easily into a health service that is highly constrained in the way it can, in the short term, reallocate resources between budgets and over time.

References

1   Hill S, Garattini S, van Loenhout J, O'Brien BJ and de Joncheere K (2003) *Technology Appraisal Programme of the National Institute for Clinical Excellence*. World Health Organization: Geneva.

2   NICE (2003) *Guide to the Methods of Technology Appraisal*. Draft for discussion at NICE Board Meeting, 19 November 2003. Available at:
www.nice.org.uk/Docref.asp?d=93882 (accessed 28.11.03).

3   Bloor K, Freemantle N, Khadjesari Z and Maynard A (2003) Impact of NICE guidance on laparoscopic surgery for inguinal hernias: analysis of interrupted time series. *British Medical Journal* **326**: 578.

4   Dent THS and Sadler M (2002) From guidance to practice: why NICE is not enough. *British Medical Journal* **324**: 842–5.

5   HM Treasury (2003) *The Green Book. Appraisal and evaluation in central government.* Available at http://greenbook.treasury.gov.uk (accessed 28.11.03).

NICE challenges

Alan Maynard

Having been involved in the creation of NICE in 1997, I regard it as an essential NHS agency and I hope it and complementary agencies can cope better with the challenges discussed below.[1]

Incremental drift in technology adoption in the NHS

The producers of new technologies continue to market unproven technologies (in terms of cost-effectiveness) directly to clinicians and other potential users. This marketing leads to the adoption of unproven interventions and technological 'creep'. This needs to be dealt with by legislation and inspected by the Commission of Healthcare Audit and Inspection, and the Foundation Hospital Regulator. Clinical experimentation with unproven technologies can not only damage patient health but also creates expenditure inflation.

Being explicit about rationing

Despite assertions to the contrary, NICE is the agent of NHS rationing.[2] Rationing is ubiquitous and involves depriving (or not offering) patients of care from which they would benefit, and which they would like to have.

The dominance of cost-effectiveness over clinical effectiveness

What is clinically effective may not be cost-effective (e.g. beta interferon for the treatment of multiple sclerosis). What is cost-effective is always clinically effective. To prioritise or ration competing therapies, it is necessary to rank them in terms of their relative cost-effectiveness. This has been the focus of many NICE appraisals, although not all of them offer explicit cost per QALY estimates as yet.

The dominance of equalising quality adjusted life years expectancy over efficiency

Beware of narrow-minded economists 'paddling' the efficiency (cost-effectiveness) canoe! The NHS was created to mitigate inequalities in health. These have increased over recent decades and can be mitigated by devising equity weights for QALYs that reflect society's desire to pursue greater equality in QALY expectancy. Such weights may reflect rich/poor, young/old and other equity considerations, e.g. Williams' 'fair innings' arguments.[3] To ignore the equity issue is to ignore the purpose of the NHS.

Processes for selecting technologies for approval

Although efforts have been made to broaden the 'church' from which appraisal suggestions are derived, there continues to be over-emphasis on new technologies and relatively little attention paid to old technologies that may be redundant. If the latter were appraised, resources would be freed to mitigate the inflationary pressure NICE imposes on the NHS.

Eliciting the preferences of a wider group of NHS managers might be helpful. Their increasing exposure to review in the 'star wars', CHI/CHAI reviews and by the Foundation Trust Regulator will make them increasingly determined to identify resource saving by identifying and eradicating useless technologies.

Constraining NICE-induced inflation

De facto the NICE 'fourth hurdle' is set, give or take £5000, at around £25 000 per QALY. This has led to NICE approval of some marginal therapies, especially in the cancer area. There are intense funding pressures in the NHS. These are exacerbated by the inflationary new contracts for GPs and consultants, the New Deal, the European Union (EU) Working Time Directive, increased National Insurance contributions and other changes that add to expenditure with little benefit in terms of service activity or quality.

The NICE hurdle is essentially arbitrary but too generous for its appraisals to be funded in the NHS. Its inflationary impact is intolerable. This problem can be addressed by:

- acquiring the preferences of NHS chief executives and using them to determine the hurdle. This would probably reduce the cut-off to £12 000–15 000 per QALY, with many more technologies failing to win NICE approval

- giving NICE a notional budget (e.g. £500 million a year) and requiring it to stay within budget
- giving NICE a real budget of £500 million per year and requiring it to stay in budget by funding implementation of all its proposals.

The third option is superior in that it would require NICE to determine the value of the QALY at the margin and also incentivise it to balance cost-adding and cost-reducing appraisals. The politics of these options would be complex and difficult. The alternative will lead to variations in the take-up of NICE advice and exacerbation of 'postcode' prescribing.

Overview

NICE is an essential NHS rationing agent. Its development requires that it and the government meet these six challenges. If this does not happen, the resultant organisation will be unable to meets its obligations, i.e. resources will be used inefficiently and the NHS will fail to reduce inequalities in quality adjusted life expectancy.

References

1   Bloor K and Maynard A (1997) Regulating the pharmaceutical industry. *British Medical Journal* **315**: 200–1.

2   Association of the British Pharmaceutical Industry (2003) *The Expert Patient*. ABPI: London. www.abpi.org.uk/publications/publication_details/expert_patient/power_point_doc_NICE.asp (accessed 14.10.03).

3   Williams A (1997) Intergenerational equity: an exploratory of the 'fair innings' argument. *Health Economics* **6 (2)**: 117–32.

Priority setting and healthcare commissioning: is there a case for a UK network?

Angela Bate, Cam Donaldson and Tony Hope

Priority setting and healthcare commissioning

Hidden among recent attention given to the development of foundation hospitals has been government recognition of the need to strengthen the role of commissioning, backing up an earlier commitment to give PCTs responsibility for this task.[1]

'Effective commissioning' is essentially about making decisions concerning the types and levels of care to be funded within a given budget in order to meet the health objectives of specific geographic populations. This is inextricably related to the task of prioritising between competing claims on these scarce resources, which has been part of the UK NHS for decades, and is now globally recognised; note the recent establishment of the International Society for Health Care Priorities.

Current debates focus on the question of how best to determine priorities.[2-4] Evidence-based approaches have been exemplified through the creation of national bodies, such as NICE, its role being to produce national guidance on individual technologies ('appraisals') and the management of specific conditions ('clinical guidelines').[5] But the question remains as to what local decision makers do with such information in their own contexts of managing scarcity. What, for example, are the local frameworks within which the products of such important national bodies are to be applied?

The role of NICE

How does NICE perform in terms of aiding priority setting? This topic has been widely discussed, with authors rising to the challenge of constructing snappy titles to include a pun on the word 'NICE'![6-10] Some of the main criticisms have been:

- NICE takes too 'mechanistic' an approach to evaluation, focusing on health outcomes in terms of QALYs and paying too little attention to other factors that should affect priorities. The NICE approach gives the impression that priority should be given to technology-related healthcare interventions, like pharmaceuticals and devices, which more obviously lend themselves to the methods that NICE adopts.
- In practice, choice must be made between alternatives, whereas NICE conducts 'one-off' evaluations. Acceptance of a technology which produces additional benefits, but at additional cost, is, at best, of partial use to decision makers working under resource constraints, choosing between alternative healthcare programmes. Indeed, it has been predicted that 'saying yes' results in either continued expansion in expenditures, or commissioners 'slavishly funding marginally cost-effective drugs approved by NICE and diverting funds away from more cost-effective existing services that lack politically powerful advocates'.[6]
- Although NICE was set up, in part, to avoid postcode prescribing, the services from which funds are diverted will vary locally so that the issue of 'equity across the country' remains.

To address these problems, something additional is required in order to make the link between national and local priorities. The recent House of Commons Health Committee Report on NICE stated that: making NICE guidance mandatory raises challenges for NHS priority setting; practical systems and structures should be put in place to improve capacity to implement guidance, as implicit prioritisation is insufficient; and the government must work towards 'a comprehensive framework for healthcare prioritisation, underpinned by an explicit set of ethical and rational values to allow the relative costs and benefits of different areas of NHS spending to be comparatively assessed in an informed way'.[1]

But what might such a framework look like and how can we ensure it conforms to ethical and economic principles while recognising both the complexities of healthcare, and what is already going on in commissioning organisations in this respect? To us, these are challenging questions which can be addressed only through the creation of a national network to share experiences and develop best practice.

The need to create a UK network

Resource scarcity will never go away and the imperative to examine local needs will always be there. NICE guidance has to be examined in this context. The commissioning task in the 'New NHS' involves trading local and national priorities, and centrally driven targets and guidance. Though currently undertaken within PCTs, the ways in which these decisions are made and the consistency in approaches are difficult to establish.

In recent years, much progress has been made, internationally, on developing frameworks, based on both economics and ethical principles, which recognise scarcity, the complexity of healthcare and, thus, the need for pragmatism to be built into priority-setting processes.[11–16] In 'evaluations' of such frameworks, managers typically stated that they allow proposed service developments to be treated equally, according to predefined criteria, and that they provide the opportunity to consider weighing-up, once development monies are spent, the relative priority of currently unfunded developments against potential areas for disinvestment.[13,14]

In the absence of NICE becoming a national healthcare rationing agency (as suggested elsewhere[6]), how can best practice in priority setting and, thus, commissioning, be developed and disseminated throughout the NHS? Such dissemination is necessary to enhance PCT capacity to effectively, efficiently and equitably receive guidance and implement targets while accounting for local needs. Moreover how can these practices be adopted routinely by commissioners? Are there the necessary information systems and incentives in order for such processes to become fully embedded within management structures and local delivery and development planning processes?

In order to meet such challenges, it is important to bring together both management and research communities in a UK network to ensure that processes are both pragmatic and based on relevant principles of economics and ethics. The result would be two main types of 'living' tools to guide local development planning: one, based on economic principles, providing a step-by-step guide to assessment of the current situation in any given PCT and how to weigh up options for change, the other providing guiding principles against which to evaluate the ethics of any process.

Conclusion

A national network as described above will help PCTs, and other commissioning bodies, to:

- implement guidance and targets while ensuring that other local needs are met and identify some serious clashes between national targets and local needs
- minimise the threat of local development monies being taken up by meeting targets based on national guidance. This can be achieved by justifying why local plans to meet targets based on national guidance might vary
- reconcile ministerial concerns for good quality across the board in the NHS with the need for local discretion on meeting claims on resources.

To do this, it is urgent to recognise first, that priority setting is integral to the delivery of healthcare and, second, that the best way forward is to create a network of expert practitioners and academics to develop and disseminate best practice in priority setting.

Acknowledgements

Cam Donaldson holds the Health Foundation Chair in Health Economics at the University of Newcastle upon Tyne and is an ESRC/EPSRC Advanced Institute of Management Research (AIM) Public Service Fellow. TH would like to acknowledge Professor Alastair Gray, Dr Jane Wolstenholme, Professor Sian Griffiths and Dr John Reynolds for many helpful discussions. The views expressed in this paper are those of the authors, not the funders or our colleagues.

References

1 The House of Commons Health Committee (2002) *Second Report of Session 2001–02 on the National Institute for Clinical Excellence. Vol 1: Report and Proceedings of the Committee* (HC 515-I). The Stationery Office: London.

2 McCulloch D (2003) Scientific prioritisation: inescapable judgement. *Applied Health Economics and Health Policy* **2 (2)**: 71–3.

3 Drummond M and Donaldson C (2003) In the land of the blind, is one-eyed economics the king? Commentary. *Applied Health Economics and Health Policy* **2 (2)**: 73–6.

4 Sassi F (2003) Setting priorities for the evaluation of health interventions: when theory does not meet practice. *Health Policy* **63**: 141–54.

5 National Institute for Clinical Excellence (2000) *Framework Document, June 2000*. NICE: London. www.nice.org.uk/Docref.asp?d = 2093

6 Cookson R, McDaid D and Maynard A (2001) Wrong SIGN, NICE mess: is national guidance distorting allocation of resources? *British Medical Journal* **323**: 742–5.

7 Birch S and Gafni A (2002) On being NICE in the UK: guidelines for technology appraisal for the NHS in England and Wales. *Health Economics* **11**: 185–91.

8 Oliver A (2002) NICE and its implications for health inequalities. *Euro Observer* **4 (2)**: 3.

9 Campbell A (2003) NICE or NASTY? Threats to justice from an emphasis on effectiveness. In: *Health Care Priority Setting: implications for health inequalities. Proceedings from a meeting of the Health Equity Network*. The Nuffield Trust: London.

10 Griffiths S (2003) Implications of priority setting on health inequalities: does NICE help at a local level? In: *Health Care Priority Setting: implications for health inequalities. Proceedings from a meeting of the Health Equity Network*. The Nuffield Trust: London.

11 Ashton T, Cumming J and Devlin N (2000) Priority-setting in New Zealand: translating principles into practice. *Journal of Health Services Research and Policy* **5 (3)**: 170–5.

12 Scott A, Currie G and Donaldson C (1998) Evaluating innovation in general practice: a pragmatic framework using programme budgeting and marginal analysis. *Family Practice* **15**: 216–22.

13 Mitton C, Donaldson C, Halma L and Gall N (2002) Setting priorities and allocating

resources in regional health authorities: a report from two pilot exercises using programme budgeting and marginal analysis. *Health Care Management FORUM* **15**: 39–47.

14   Mitton C and Donaldson C (2003) Setting priorities and allocating resources in health regions: lessons from a project evaluating program budgeting and marginal analysis (PBMA). *Health Policy* **64**: 333–48.

15   Daniels N and Sabin J (1998) The ethics of accountability in managed care reform. *Health Affairs* **17**: 50–64.

16   Hope T, Reynolds J and Griffiths S (2002) Rationing decisions: integrating cost-effectiveness with other values. In: R Rhodes, MP Battin and A Silvers (eds) *Medicine and Social Justice: essays on the distribution of health care*. Oxford University Press: New York and Oxford.

Who has the responsibility for picking up the research agenda?

Chris Counsell

The title for this talk was given in advance by the organisers of the conference and perhaps reflects a perception that the changes in the legal and organisational framework for research in the NHS is leading to a fundamental change in the drivers for research. Whether or not this is true is one question, whether or not there ought to be a change is another. Certainly, NHS organisations have to take the governance of research more seriously than before and not all non-NHS researchers have fully recognised this changed environment. But this does not automatically mean that R&D is any more important to NHS managers or that they are interested in driving research in their organisation.

The NHS, like all healthcare systems, relies heavily on technological advancement and innovation – new techniques, new drugs, new devices, new ways of working. In industries where innovation is important to keep ahead of competitors, R&D is actively built into the business plans. This appears not to be so in the NHS. The following are some possible reasons.

Support costs

Until the reforms of 1991 and the establishment of an R&D Directorate within the Department of Health, research happened in the NHS without any great planning or strategic purpose. The reforms were supposed to change all of that with a National Director of R&D and supporting team in the Department of Health, together with regional offices to put into effect locally the strategy agreed nationally. The subsequent changes in the funding arrangements in the wake of the Culyer report meant that R&D was apparently secure financially and strategically. But arguably, R&D has not noticeably benefited as a result, since outside its compartment, in mainstream NHS management, R&D can safely be ignored. Although R&D spending has not fallen in real terms, it has not increased to match the overall increase in NHS funding in recent years. There was once a target for R&D expenditure to exceed 1.5% of total NHS expenditure. In fact R&D now accounts for less than 1% of total NHS spending and is continuing to fall. Moreover, apart from minor tinkering at the edges, the allocation of the budget to individual NHS Trusts has been locked at the relative values declared in 1996 regardless of any subsequent changes in the quantity or quality of research activity.

Research costs

Although a substantial amount of research is carried out on NHS patients using NHS facilities, the majority of research is simply done *to* the NHS or for the NHS (in the sense that it is good for it), rather than with the NHS or even by the NHS. The majority of healthcare-related research funding is channelled through the Universities. The Association of Medical Research Charities has noted that less than 2% of the research funds from its members are awarded to NHS organisations. Research Council funding and even DoH research funds are overwhelmingly allocated to Universities. There is little opportunity for NHS organisations to have their direct research costs considered in the funding. Moreover, the research priorities of academic institutions can occasionally be at odds with the clinical needs of the NHS locally, regionally or nationally.

Infrastructure

NHS organisations have limited access to dedicated funds for facilities and infrastructure to support research – such as laboratories, pharmacies, IT, or clinical trials management facilities. Routine clinical facilities are often over-stretched and are not always adequate for specialist research needs. Extending these facilities for research use is likely to be more cost-effective than funding dedicated facilities but this is rarely considered.

Research *and* development?

Like industry, and unlike academia, the NHS is both a producer and an end-user of research. So not only should the NHS know what research it needs, but it should also have the means to implement the results of the research. In practice though, NHS R&D is mainly concerned with the 'R' side of R&D. The criteria for judging the quality of R&D are very much research focused – peer-reviewed, original, generalisable, publishable, externally funded. The majority of external funding is only focused on the research end of the spectrum. This gives the impression that 'R' is valued while 'D' is not. In industry, R&D usually stands for research and development, in the NHS R&D tends to stand for research, the '&D' is silent. Development activity clearly does occur but it is not overtly co-ordinated in the way research is.

In immediate resource terms R&D is of little positive relevance to NHS managers and there is therefore little incentive for them to consider the needs of R&D. Given all of this it seems unlikely that NHS Trusts will pick up the research agenda. Foundation Hospital Trusts could change all of that if, like industry, the management sees thriving R&D activity as essential for driving forward the business. However, a more widely held fear seems to be that the converse is likely to be true and that R&D will be of even less relevance than now.

What has happened in recent years is an increase in regulation of the governance of research through the DoH's Research Governance Framework and the EU Directive on Clinical Trials. These recognise that researchers, employers, funders, sponsors and healthcare providers all have distinct roles and as a consequence have raised the profile of NHS Trusts in this process. Trusts are responsible for the care of the patients that could be compromised by any research that interferes with established clinical practice. While in the past NHS Trusts didn't seem to know what research was being done on its patients, now the Chief Executives are legally accountable for the impact of the research.

Does it matter? A cynic might say that research (and development) continues in the NHS despite everything that has happened in the past 10 years rather than because of it. New drugs, devices and techniques are introduced into the NHS. But research does not appear to be a primary business driver for any healthcare system around the world. If R&D were taken more seriously by mainstream NHS management would that lead to more rapid improvements in the quality of the service provided?

If the NHS is not driving research, who is? It remains predominantly the researchers themselves. Funding priorities may change – the DoH is linking theirs increasingly to the National Service Frameworks – but it relies on the same researchers to carry the programmes forward and sit on the same committees that decide the allocation of research funds.

Index

abdominal aortic aneurysm, uncertainty 12
accountability, policy making 172
advocacy, patients 118–19
appraisals
  HTA 15–17
  NICE 14–17, 138–41
assessment
  interventional procedures 22–4
  see also health technology assessment;
    Multidisciplinary Assessment of
    Technology Centre for Health;
    Technology Appraisal Guidance
audiologists' role, ENT 129–30
audit
  cancer services 139–40
  CHAI 56, 61–3
  CHI 79–80
  clinical audits 139–40
  EFM 142–8
  National Clinical Audit 98–101
  NICE 142–8
aural care clinic, ENT 128–30

Barnet and Chase Farm Hospitals Trust,
    failure to meet targets 132–4
barriers
  medicine taking 65
  policy making 172–3
'best practice', CHI 77–81
Blackburn Royal Infirmary, ENT 126–31

Calman–Hine initiative, cancer services
    policy making 176–7
cancer services
  Calman–Hine initiative 176–7
  clinical audits 139–40
  clinical governance 140
  consent form audit 140
  funding 139
  implementation framework 138
  Improving Outcomes project 177

NICE TAG 138–41
  policy making 176–80
  service organisation 178–9
  using evidence 177–8
capacity measures, ENT 130
cardiac rehabilitation 123–5
Care Standards Act (2000) 61
career enhancement 149–51
CDM *see* chronic disease management
CEMACH *see* Confidential Enquiry into
    Maternal and Child Health
CHAI *see* Commission for Healthcare Audit
    and Inspection
change, sustainable 40–2
Changing Workforce Programme (CWP)
  nursing innovations 120–2
  quality improvements 120–2
CHD *see* coronary heart disease
CHI *see* Commission for Health Improvement
child health, CEMACH 43–6
chronic disease management (CDM) 51–4
clinical effectiveness, NICE 188
clinical governance
  cancer services 140
  case summaries 88–90
  corporate initiative 86
  front line 95–7
  laughter therapy 89–90
  physiotherapists 88–9
  pocket guide 112–17
  RAID 95–7
  strategic approach 85–91
  trust suggestion scheme 86–7
  ward visit programme 87–8
Clinical Guidelines Implementation Group
    109–11
clinical performance, measuring 55–7
  arguments in favour 55
  drawbacks 56
  intervention 133–4
  star ratings impact 132–4

clinical trials *see* trials, clinical/controlled
Commission for Healthcare Audit and
    Inspection (CHAI)
  clinical performance, measuring 56
  private sector 61–3
Commission for Health Improvement (CHI)
  audit 79–80
  'best practice' 77–81
  key action areas 136–7
  recommendations into practice 135–7
  study 77–9
commitment
  quality management 41
  social care services 71
compliance/non-compliance, medicine
    taking 64–8
concordance, medicine taking, Task Force
    on Medicines Partnership 64–8
Confidential Enquiry into Maternal and
    Child Health (CEMACH) 43–6
  child health 45
  continuity elements 43
  current programmes 44–6
  diabetes in pregnancy 45
  maternal enquiry 44–5
  NICE guidelines 44
  perinatal mortality data 45
  programme development 43–4
  Project 27/28; 45
consensus recommendations
  formulating 18–21
  guideline development 18–19
  methods 18–19
  NCC 20–1
  nominal group technique 19
  novel approaches 19–21
  Pearson Process 19–20
consent form audit, cancer services 140
consumer involvement, trials, clinical/
    controlled 162–4
contract, GMS 51–4
controlled trials *see* trials, clinical/controlled
coronary heart disease (CHD), rehabilitation
    123–5
cost-effectiveness analyses
  health economics 185–7
  NICE 188
cost/quality-adjusted life years, technology
    assessment 183–4, 188–9

decision making
  evidence role 182–4
  HTA 14–17
  local 183–4
  NICE 182–4
  policies 14–17
demand measures, ENT 130
depression, uncertainty 12
development
  career enhancement 149–51
  skills 149–51
diabetes care
  new roles 122
  nursing innovations 120–2
  quality improvements 120–2
diabetes in pregnancy, CEMACH 45
diagnostic uncertainty 11
Donabedian, A 53

Ear, Nose and Throat (ENT) 126–31
  audiologists' role 129–30
  aural care clinic 128–30
  capacity measures 130
  demand measures 130
  follow-up 127
  ideas 126
  nursing role 126–8
  process maps 130
  tonsillectomy 127–8
  waiting list times 130–1
economics, health *see* health economics
electronic fetal monitoring (EFM) 142–8
  education 146
  equipment 146
  FBS 147–8
  IA 143–5
  monitors 146
  outcome measures 147
  staff self-audit 148
  staff training 146
  women's perceptions 145
emergency care
  quality agenda 38–9
  targets 38–9
ENT *see* Ear, Nose and Throat
evidence gap, size 11–13
evidence, research, patients'/public's role
    25–7

evidence role
    cancer services policy making 176–80
    decision making 182–4
    market access 178–9, 183–4
    policy making 171–80

facilitators, policy making 172–3
failure, star ratings impact 132–4
fetal blood sampling (FBS) 147–8
fetal monitoring, NICE guidelines 142–8
Fine, M, SCIE 35–7

General Medical Services (GMS), contract
    51–4
guideline development, consensus
    recommendations 18–19

Health and Social Care Advisory Service
    (HASCAS) 106–8
healthcare commissioning
    mental health 106–8
    NICE 191–2
    UK network 191–5
health economics
    cost-effectiveness analyses 185–7
    recommendations role 185–7
    solutions 186–7
health inequalities 92–4
    themes 93–4
health technology assessment (HTA)
    approaches 13–17
    decision making 14–17
    NICE appraisals 14–17
heart failure, uncertainty 12
homicide, National Confidential Inquiry
    47–50
HTA *see* health technology assessment
hypercholesterolaemia, uncertainty 13

IA *see* intermittent auscultation
Improving Outcomes project, cancer services
    177
inequalities *see* health inequalities
inflation, NICE 189–90
*Informing Judgment: case studies of health
    policy and research in six countries* 172
intermittent auscultation (IA), EFM
    143–5

interventional procedures
    assessment 22–4
    benefits 22–4
    clinical performance, measuring 133–4
    national registry 23–4
Interventional Procedures Programme
    168–70
investment, quality management 40

joint working, SCIE 35–7

laughter therapy, clinical governance
    89–90
Leeds North West PCT, cardiac rehabilitation
    123–5
Liberating the Talents 52
Lind, James
    legacy 3–8
    relevance 5–8
local decision making 183–4

market access, evidence role 178–9,
    183–4
MATCH *see* Multidisciplinary Assessment of
    Technology Centre for Health
maternal enquiry, CEMACH 44–5
maternal health, CEMACH 43–6
medicine taking
    barriers 65
    concordance 64–8
    public attitudes 65–6
mental health commissioning 106–8
mental illness, National Confidential Inquiry
    into Suicide and Homicide by People
    with Mental Illness 47–50
Multidisciplinary Assessment of Technology
    Centre for Health (MATCH) 28–31
    conceptual view 29
    critical links 28–30
    impact 30–1
    introduction to 28

National Care Standards Commission
    (NCSC), private sector 61–3
National Clinical Audit
    2002–2004; 98–101
    future work 100–1
    strengthening 99–100

National Clinical Governance Support
Programme for Stroke 103
National Collaborating Centre for Cancer
(NCCC) 20–1
National Collaborating Centre for Health
Technology Assessment (NCCHTA) 15
National Confidential Inquiry into Suicide
and Homicide by People with Mental
Illness 47–50
new directions 49–50
recent findings 48–9
National Institute for Clinical Excellence
(NICE)
appraisals 14–17
appraisals, HTA 14–17
appraisals, TAG 138–41
audit 142–8
cancer services 138–41
CEMACH 44
challenges 188–90
clinical effectiveness 188
cost-effectiveness analyses 188
decision making 182–4
EFM 142–8
guidance implementation 109–11,
169–70
guidelines audit 142–8
healthcare commissioning 191–2
HTA 15–17
inflation 189–90
Interventional Procedures Programme
169–70
NICE TAG 138–41
policy making 171–5
priority setting 191–2
QALYs 188–9
rationing 188
technology assessment 138–41, 188–90
national registry, interventional procedures
23–4
National Service Frameworks (NSFs),
emergency care 39
NCCC see National Collaborating Centre for
Cancer
NCCHTA see National Collaborating Centre
for Health Technology Assessment
NCSC see National Care Standards
Commission
network, UK see UK network

NHS
four nations delivering 58–60
Wales 58–60
NICE see National Institute for Clinical
Excellence
NICE TAG see Technology Appraisal
Guidance
nominal group technique, consensus
recommendations 19
NSFs see National Service Frameworks
nursing innovations, quality improvements
via 120–2
nursing role, ENT 126–8

partnership
NICE guidance 109–11
SCIE 35–7
social care services 72
patient and public involvement (PPI)
102–5, 118–19
patients
advocacy 118–19
involvement 102–5, 118–19, 158–64
role, research evidence 25–7
trials, clinical/controlled 160–1
waiting list times 130–1
Pearson Process, consensus
recommendations 19–20
performance, measuring clinical see clinical
performance, measuring
perinatal mortality data, CEMACH 45
pharmaceutical industry, trials, clinical/
controlled 158–61
pharmacy department, risk management
82–4
physiotherapists, clinical governance
88–9
pocket guide, clinical governance 112–17
flowcharts 112–14
impact, patient care 116
index 115
language 115–16
outcomes 116
project 112–13
sharing learning 116–17
toolkit component 113–15
policies
perspectives 14–17
pressures 14–17

policy making
  accountability 172
  barriers 172–3
  cancer services 176–80
  evidence role 171–80
  facilitators 172–3
  *Informing Judgment: case studies of health
    policy and research in six countries*
    172
  realities 174
  relationships 173
  research role 171–80
PPI *see* patient and public involvement
primary care, standards 51–4
Princess Anne Hospital, fetal monitoring
    142–8
priority setting
  NICE 191–2
  UK network 191–5
private sector
  CHAI 61–3
  inspecting 58–60
  NCSC 61–3
prognostic uncertainty 11
progressive quality management 40–2
Project 27/28, CEMACH 45
prostate testing for cancer and treatment
    (ProtectT study) 155–7
ProtectT study 155–7
public
  involvement 102–5, 118–19
  role, research evidence 25–7
public attitudes, medicine taking 65–6

quality adjusted life years (QALYs)
  NICE 188–9
  technology assessment 183–4
quality agenda
  emergency care 38–9
  patient/public involvement 102–5
  stroke services 102–5
  targets impact 38–9
quality improvements, via nursing
    innovations 120–2
quality management
  building blocks 41–2
  commitment 41
  investment 40
  progressive 40–2

resources 41
role modelling 41

R&D *see* research and development
RAID *see* review, agree, implement,
    demonstrate
ratings
  intervention 133–4
  policy/practice 132–3
  star ratings impact 132–4
  see also clinical performance, measuring
rationing, NICE 188
recommendations into practice, CHI
    135–7
Reforming Emergency Care 38–9
registry, interventional procedures 23–4
renewal, clinical performance intervention
    134
replacement, clinical performance
    intervention 133
research agenda
  costs 196–8
  infrastructure 197
  R&D 197–8
  responsibility 196–8
research and development (R&D) 197–8
research role
  cancer services policy making 176–80
  policy making 171–80
resources, quality management 41
retrenchment, clinical performance
    intervention 133–4
review, agree, implement, demonstrate
    (RAID) 95–7
risk management, pharmacy department
    82–4
role modelling, quality management 41

SCIE *see* Social Care Institute for Excellence
scurvy 3–5
service organisation, cancer services
    178–9
skills development 149–51
Social Care Institute for Excellence (SCIE)
    35–7
  framework 36–7
  results 37
social care services 69–73
  conflict 72

consultancy 72
current knowledge 70
diversity 72–3
expectations 72
feedback 70–1
impact, service user participation 69–73
improving 69–73
individual level participation/change
    71
marginalisation 72–3
messages, policy/practice 69–70
organisational commitment/
    responsiveness 71
participation benefits 70
partnership 72
power relations 71–2
Southampton University Hospitals NHS
    Trust, fetal monitoring 142–8
standards
    Care Standards Act (2000) 61
    primary care 51–4
    raising 51–4
star ratings impact, failure 132–4
stroke services
    experiences, programme 104–5
    patient/public involvement 102–5
    quality agenda 102–5
    user involvement 103–4
suicide
    diagnoses 48–9
    methods 48
    National Confidential Inquiry 47–50
sustainable change 40–2
systematic reviews 4, 5–7

Tackling Health Inequalities 92–4
targets
    emergency care 38–9
    failure to meet 132–4
    impact 38–9
    star ratings impact 132–4
Task Force on Medicines Partnership
    areas of work 66–7
    concordance, medicine taking 64–8
Technology Appraisal Guidance (NICE TAG)
    138–41

technology assessment
    cost/quality adjusted life years 183–4,
        188–9
    NICE 138–41, 188–90
    see also health technology assessment;
        Multidisciplinary Assessment of
        Technology Centre for Health;
        Technology Appraisal Guidance
therapeutic uncertainty 11
tonsillectomy, ENT 127–8
trials, clinical/controlled
    complex protocol design 158–9
    conduct 155–7
    consumer involvement 162–4
    design 155–7, 162–4
    first 4
    heterogeneous trial populations 165–7
    improving acceptability 26–7
    improving relevance 26
    involving participants 155–7
    management 162–4
    patient involvement 158–66
    patient pool 160–1
    poor site selection 159–60
    ProtectT study 155–7
    relevance 6–7

UK network
    healthcare commissioning 191–5
    priority setting 191–5
uncertainty
    classes 11
    diagnostic 11
    prognostic 11
    therapeutic 11
user involvement, stroke services 103–4

waiting list times, ENT 130–1
Wales
    clinical governance 85–91
    NHS 58–60
    patient advocacy 118–19
Workforce Development Confederation
    (WDC), NICE guidance 110–11